Silver Linings

Silver Linings

FINDING GROWTH WITHIN DYSFUNCTION

Jacob Fry

Learn more about this book and the author's journey at
www.evolvedandelevated.com

ISBN: 9798484489831 (paperback)

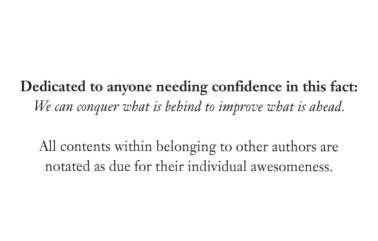

Dedicated to anyone needing confidence in this fact:
We can conquer what is behind to improve what is ahead.

All contents within belonging to other authors are
notated as due for their individual awesomeness.

Contents

How to Navigate this Book

Each chapter is a true story (many stories are omitted, but those with purposeful life lessons are shared) pulled from a section in my journey.

I attempted to make the journey read in a linear format, beginning with the beginning, and ending with the present.

Throughout each chapter, some passages will be marked with a * the * represents a Silver Lining lesson that stemmed from that experience.

Each chapter will end with a "Silver Linings" section that shares some of the life lessons I gained from that experience.

The book began as a "personal journey journal" to navigate and accept my past. After finding several valuable lessons throughout I wanted to share it with others. My true hope is that sharing this will not only push me forward the past – but also show that the past can be conquered. And that the future may be anything we design it to be.

Introduction

Consider for a Moment that each event in your life occurs because the universe or a higher power is trying to guide you indirectly. Provoke you even, to realize your best self. Let's start with a reflection on what we "know."

Reflect on the extreme impossibility that you, or I, as a conscious being, even exist. Without diving into the still massively unknown variable that life is – let's talk current science. Out of hundreds of millions of potential conceptions, you were the only one to survive the trek to the egg and create life! You may decide to call it a lucky roll of the cosmic dice, but I am convinced that there is much more to this journey than luck.

Our individual journeys are much like that original journey to the egg. We are released into a world of unknowns, racing to the proverbial finish line, hoping to "win" life. Our individual life journey is littered with numerous epic adventures, peaks of adrenaline, valleys of suffering, all of which we (you) are the protagonist. In our individual story, we are the one, the most important individual in our lives.

Did you know we share the planet with 7.67 billion humans? Yet, we still navigate life as if our daily monologue is the ultimate. Each of us faces our own individual trials, fights our own demons, and does our best to continue putting one foot in front of the other every day. And yet, almost universally, we cover our hardships with the help of a mask we have built up over a lifetime of experiences.

However, there are those who have elevated their mindset and recognized that not only is this life a gift – it is an opportunity. An opportunity to relish in every Moment. An opportunity to drop the mask, accept our past, accept our failings, and conquer the conditioning that often dictates our life path. When that conditioning is conquered, and the other 7.67 billion individuals are recognized for the miracle they also are, our approach to life shifts.

We understand that all other sentient beings suffer, love, anger, endure trials, and battle with their own ego. The situational experiences vary, but the emotions, the physical sensation, and consciousness of being are universal. These universal experiences are the same regardless of geographical location, and language spoken, the religion followed, skin pigment, or any other differentiating variable. Despite different foundations and different resources, we still navigate our journeys with the same overall emotions, senses, and functions. The billionaire flying a rocket still experiences the same emotions as the family trying to scrounge to pay the rent.

I have been blessed to have suffered enough to appreciate the better things in life. Lucky enough to have had my heart broken enough to enjoy love and struggled hard enough to enjoy relaxation. Happiness is immeasurable without something sad to contrast it against. I was once an individual that was controlled by my ego. This led to significant unnecessary suffering in both mind and body. When one is focused on their individual suffering, the world becomes a dark place.

In making the shift from a suffering internally-focused ego to a grateful externally focused individual – my entire life changed. I transformed my health, intelligence, and wealth. My finances, relationships, and self-appreciation all shifted in a positive direction. Each day became a love affair with me and the world. Having this shift in knowing, I want to do all I can to help others open their minds to the gift of life and share the abundance I found in my personal journey.

If you follow the scientific perspective, you are a grand impossibility (odd of conception) within a colossal improbability (creation of life). If you believe in grand creation, then this life was gifted to you for a purpose, and you should indeed relish in each Moment. If you are agnostic, no matter, you may change your mind down the road, and if not, at minimum, you will likely find a handful of interesting stories in the pages that follow.

For myself, after navigating a few loops in the roller coaster, we call life – I sincerely believe that this life is a miraculous gift. I believe we each have the ability to become the best individual possible tomorrow if we will only accept this gift, conquer the past, adopt a growth mindset, and work diligently today.

The pages follow my personal journey from conception

to the present. Life required numerous failures, days of darkness, and some hopeless drifting to finally break my ego enough to push me to seek more. My experiences within are not all family-friendly, and this is an upfront warning to be aware of this dynamic.

Additionally, please know that while this book covers many of the dark Moments in the journey – I did not lack some pretty awe-inspiring Moments. The intention of this book is to lift the mask some and reveal the half less portrayed to the public in our journey. It is to reveal the false truths imprinted upon us, especially troubled youth, that we are limited, or our world is limited. I recall navigating mental illnesses that impacted close family, addictions that ruined lives, pain suffered needlessly, and family that seemed more like enemies. Numerous experiences that appear dysfunctional and traumatizing at first glance, when held under the microscope of a growth mindset, hold within themselves a valuable lesson to help us elevate our life at another point in time.

After all, as children, we can only see as far as others allow us to see

Conception

I n the year 1992, two beings, whom I will not name to protect their integrity, made each other's acquaintance at an alcoholics anonymous meeting. "Mom" and "Dad" were sitting within an ad-hoc circle, formed to create an open setting and encourage open discussion. The attention of the group was centered on Mom. She was a young woman, 16 years of age, with bright blue eyes and long blonde hair. She was telling the story of her personal experience with alcohol and the problems it had brought into her life up until that point.

Her father was an alcoholic who spent much of his time in local bars. In fact, at one point as a young child, she recalled he had owned a small bar, and she would sneak sips of beer from unwitting patrons. She had spent the last couple of years in a foster home, her life a general mess after her parents split up. Her father had moved onto another woman, had another daughter, and overall was content without her in his life.

Despite this dynamic, she craved her father's love, and this became a pattern for her later in life. A few years ago, she had overdosed on pills and alcohol. This event earned her a bed in foster care. She began sneaking out of her foster home and getting into trouble. She was drinking and began experimenting with drugs at an early age. The foster home relocated her to Clinton, IL, from her hometown in Quincy, IL. The goal was to get her away from the "bad crowds" she knew and the family dysfunction. Without other outlets to help her ease the troubles in her life – she attempted leaning on alcohol to help ease the individual suffering she felt due to the lack of stability in her life. This had brought her to the A.A. meeting, a requirement of her new foster home.

The group thanked her for sharing her story, and after a brief pause, Dad introduced himself. He was a soldier, currently doing national guard non-active-duty service following his return from an active-duty deployment in Germany. He had first been introduced to alcohol as a teenager as well. His justification for drinking early in life was that if he was old enough to serve, he was old enough to be served. But alcohol had become a controlling factor in his life. He found himself buying case after case of beer regularly. The attraction to alcohol was causing visible disruption in his life.

Something about the mutually shared suffering between Mom and Dad brought them together that night. Mom was attracted to the soldier, a uniform similar to one her father had worn in the past. Dad was always seeking to be the hero, wanting to save her from the unnecessary pain in her life. The two had a platonic relationship for a couple of years until Mom became an adult and was released from foster care. Moving back to Quincy, Mom returned to her hometown. Dad chased her –

Dad convinced Mom to move in with him back in the area they had met. She loved him, and he loved her – it was difficult for her to say no. Living together, they made the decision they wanted to have a family. Out of millions of potential personalities, out of numerous possible beings that could have been conceived, that specific day, I was 1 in millions of combatants fighting for the egg, and I won!

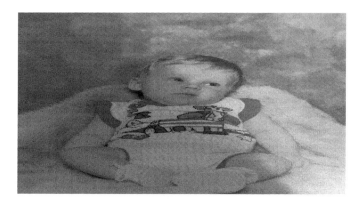

Baby Jacob Fry

Mom and Dad both did their best to create and maintain an environment that would be ideal for welcoming their miracle into the world. In May of 1993, I was removed from Mom's belly via c-section. As I was pulled into the world, Mom was pushed into depression. As the dust settled, life around the homestead began to develop patterns, and Mom missed the spontaneity of her life in her hometown. Mom was unable to continue at the current pace and decided to take a sabbatical of sorts to visit her family.

Leaving me with Dad and her mother-in-law (who happened to be an excellent Sunday school teacher), Mom left to visit with "family" and "friends." These two words have a special emphasis for Mom because, in most situations, they are generally positive influences in one's life; but for Mom, friends and family were often issuing her regular servings of un-due suffering. As such, during her trip home, she immediately broke her sobriety. Not only drinking but indulging in some serious drug abuse. So serious that she would not return to see me nor Dad for nearly a month. When she did finally make the trek home, unknown to her, she was carrying another miracle, my baby brother.

Mom was unable to revert back into the rhythm of life with Dad and me. The roller coaster of emotions she experienced in Quincy had been swimming in her mind, reminding her of her dull home life. The desire to escape the mundane led to extreme tension between my parents. These stand-offs led to unnecessary emotional damage to them both. The daily struggle of working at a factory, trying to keep family finances stable, and juggling Mom's mood swings became overwhelming for Dad. He desired an escape too, and unfortunately, the best escape he knew of was alcohol. The return of alcoholism to the house brought further negativity into their world.

Not too much time later, Mom had sick spells, and a reality check caught up with her. She was significantly late in having her menstrual period. Following a handful of doctor visits, coupled with the lacking intimacy in their relationship, it was clear to them both that the child was not Dad's. Realizing this truth, a rift began growing between them both. Dad torn, broken-hearted. Mom regretful, guilt abundant. Yet, they mutually agreed that my brother would enter into this world as Dad's son. My mother, eternally grateful, for in truth, she was not sure who was my brothers' father was, and until this day, we still do not know nor care.

Fast forward about a year past my brothers' conception. Mom was regularly visiting "home" and "family" again. She was escaping her home life with long nights and hard drugs. On one return home, visibly drained from her self-abuse, Dad issued an ultimatum. Stay with him, get clean, return to A.A. together, or separate. Dad was a strong man, but he still had a breaking point. He could not bear to see the damage Mom inflicted on herself, nor the resentment she carried regarding her life situation.

He could not handle her disappearances, sometimes weeks, unknown to him her whereabouts or assurance of safety. Mom had been seeking an escape route for some time, her mind firmly under the control of her vices. Mom chose to leave and to move back home – with my brother and me. A joint custody agreement was put into place. We would only spend summertime with Dad for the next decade or so.

SILVER LININGS

• • •

- It is easy to fall into "ruts" when life becomes a repeating pattern. These ruts can lead to a loss of interest in the daily experience of life. Be sure to shake things up; just as with juices, separation is natural.
- Numbing the impact of pain with external Band-Aids (drugs, alcohol, food) often leads to a situation worse than the one we were originally seeking to avoid.

Early Childhood

om headed for Quincy, IL, her hometown, brother, and I in tow. We would call Quincy our home for the next ten years until the impact of Mom's life choices caught up to her.

Mom never really worked for income. She would wash dishes here, clean up there, babysit, or do other odd jobs occasionally. At a young age, she was put on disability, and we survived on food stamps, Medicaid, and any other government welfare programs available. During our childhood, my brother and I, following Mom's lead, lived in nearly every section-8 applicable living space within the city border. Mom had been evicted several times throughout our younger years, forcing frequent relocation.

From noise complaints, drug abuse, and too many police visits to the inability to pay rent, keeping the same living space for a long period was a rarity. Due to the pattern of monetary-related evictions and living on government funds, the government decided she was unfit to control her own income. Mom was assigned a court-appointed counselor, a treasurer of sorts, who would issue "allowance" from her funds after the main responsibilities were covered.

This inability to spend funds as desired, on tobacco, drugs, liquor, on her vices – created a severe pain point. Mom was very creative and resourceful when it came to resolving her personal pain points. When up against a wall, she would often find a way to move forward. Unfortunately, her solution for this particular problem had a heavy impact on her children's day-to-day lives.

Mom began selling food stamps for cash and diverting child support funds to her habits. Our home quickly moved from an abundance of food to scarcity. Naturally requiring sustenance, we began finding creative avenues to stay fed. We would go to local food pantries and eat as many soup kitchen free lunches as were available. We did not starve, but we certainly did not have the ability to be choosy in our meal options. With Mom using child support intended for clothing and school supplies, my brother and I were often spotted in hand-me-downs or shopping with Mom at the Salvation Army for clothes. *

The moral of the story? We were raised with little and became comfortable without. Yet, we still desired more and were often envious of other children that had new shoes or the latest gadget. This type of environment (poverty, wanting, feeling of lack) tends to push individuals to take any and all opportunity that presents itself. This was especially apparent in regard to Mom's choice of mates. Mom could generally burn through a few relationships every year, never truly creating anything of substance – most of the connections being formed in the "here for a good time, not a long time" mindset. The first memory I have is courtesy of one of Mom's mates on my 7th birthday.

SILVER LININGS

• • •

- Frugality is a great boon in growing a sturdy personal finance foundation. I still shop and find very nice clothing for pennies on the dollar at Salvation Army and goodwill stores. Look like a million bucks for a few quarters!

Buzzcut

I had strategically placed a whoopie cushion under a couch cushion in the living room. I sat, waiting anxiously for an unexpecting victim to plop down and release a fake fluctuation. My uncle was the victim, a jest himself, he sat down on the couch, and the cushion let out a potent farting sound. With a lighthearted laugh, he pressed on gleefully, playing with what he referred to as a "fart bag." This Moment was a joyful experience for me as a child. One that was unfortunately overshadowed when the party attendees departed.

During this time, Mom was dating a gentleman whom most would refer to as a "skinhead." S.H., for short, S.H. took it upon himself to give the birthday boy and his brother a buzzcut. Which I recall being some form of harmless indoctrination from his point of view; it was a devastating idea from mine. I was rather fond of my hair and did not like the thought of looking like S.H. I rejected the "offer," and the topic was dropped with little resistance.

S.H. had another beer and then another...and another. S.H. was prone to violence and aggression while intoxicated. After a few beers, he revisited the suggestion, except this time, it was a demand. I was playing with a toy car that was gifted to me early that day – when S.H. picked me up by my arm and forced me to a kitchen chair. Tears began streaming down my face. I did not want the haircut and besides, wasn't it my birthday? Shouldn't this be my day?

I was quickly brought back to reality when S.H. began berating me. "STOP BEING A PUSSY" he yelled. "Stop crying like a little fag". He laughed at my tears over my "sissy hair." I can still feel his dark intention and need for control. His eyes wide and his muscles tense, he turned on the clippers. Mom was in the kitchen, also drinking, softly reminding S.H. to be gentle and not to be so rough. Gripping me firmly, he made his first pass over my head. I was fighting hard not to sob*, as I truly feared what S.H. might do in his current state.

My brother, watching the entire event from the next room, glanced into my eyes. He was frightened. He was saddened, but not for himself. He has always been an empath, always having love for others and concerning more for others' needs than his own. His eyes revealed his concern, the corner of his lips curled down in a sympathetic frown as his eyes also began to well up. Finally, S.H. was satisfied with his work and ordered me to get up. Inviting my brother over, he began his trek over and had cleared up his tears before sitting down. Always one to handle emotional events with relative grace. S.H. had us sweep up "our mess" as he returned to another beer. He expressed his gratitude that no more "homo haircuts" were in the house.

This experience instilled in me the fear of showing emotion to others. For years, stemming from this single experience, I would not cry in front of others, and also rarely when alone. This false construct that emotions caused pain would not be destroyed until nearly two decades later. In full transparency, fleshing out this scene to paper and accepting this truth is one of the more emotional experiences of my life to date. Unfortunately for us, as well as for Moms' stability, the men in her life never really raised the bar S.H. set.

Jacob & Brother Christmas time

SILVER LININGS

● ● ●

- I learned how to exert control over my emotions during this experience. That has been a helpful tool throughout life – from controlling anger when someone is instigating to controlling excitement when negotiating a vehicle purchase. Control of emotions is a great boon.

Drugs are Bad

A year or so later, Mom met Vietnamese twins. V1 and V2 were their names. For a while, they both lived with us (rent-free, of course). The twins were quite literally professional con artists, always seeking to hustle, rob, steal, and deal for a dollar. They were both excellent pool sharks, and as a young child, I thought their personal pool sticks were the coolest thing since bagged chips.

On one or two occasions, I had the chance to watch them play pool for cash bets at a local bar. They would intentionally play bad and lose at a low-wagered game or two, and when someone worked up the confidence to bet big, they would run the table. After long nights of bar hopping with their pockets full of cash, they would retire before their "jobs" the next morning. I must admit, there is one thing these two had over other "men" in Mom's life, and that was their work ethic and relentlessness.

Mom dated V1 for quite some time. He was a serious drug addict, his favorite drug to abuse being crack cocaine. He and Mom would spend numerous days smoking and just zoning out in the apartment. It was the strangest thing to witness as a child. They would just sit stoned face, picking at the kitchen table or floor, seeming to endlessly pursue some thought just beyond their grasp.

Their habit cost serious cash to sustain and coupled with V1's gambling addiction; household funds were often in extreme fluctuation. One week they would be worry-free, the next arguments galore as they figured out how to get a "fix." V1 eventually expanded his horizons into meth manufacturing. They were setting up a makeshift lab in Mom's basement. Mom had a cellar under the apartment we were in at the time. I remember stumbling upon a table in the cellar that was surrounded by empty cold medicine boxes and hosted several different pieces of "lab equipment." At the time, I did not really understand the seriousness of the events taking place in the basement. I remember V1 proudly proclaiming that he would make thousands of dollars each month.

If it weren't for the drug addiction and gambling habit, V1 could have accumulated some serious money. He could have helped stock the pantry with some food. But rather than save or provide, the money was always flushed away at the riverboat casino or catching the next high. It wasn't too long before someone caught onto what was occurring in that cellar. V1 was caught up in a raid and was issued a lengthy prison sentence* as he already had a criminal record. Mom was considered a lesser accomplice, seeing a short jail sentence, of which my brother and I stayed with our grandfather.

It was tragic for my brother and me – Mom was all we knew, and it was difficult not understanding why this was happening. When she was released, despite forced sobriety, she was smoking cigarettes and drinking that same night again. Even after some time off the hard stuff, she found her way back to it as well. Mom found a new place, and we were back together in no time.

SILVER LININGS

• • •

- Often, shortcuts will lead to devastating long-term consequences. Take a shortcut to wealth illegally, and you'll be rewarded with a prison sentence. Take the longer path that requires self-growth and effort – you will likely find many rewards along that path.

If You Play With Fire…

D uring this period of our life, Mom was absent from most of our day-to-day adventures. She was present but just absent, tied up in drug-seeking, drinking, and other escapism. One morning, famished, I decided to make my brother and me bacon for breakfast. I had never cooked on a stove in my life, but after attempting to wake Mom for an hour, we were starving (at least we thought we were).

Turning on the burner, I placed the skillet over the flame and tossed on the frozen bacon (yes, frozen). I was not really tall enough to reach the pan and struggled to effectively turn over the bacon. After cooking for a little while, the grease had begun to build up in the pan. It was bubbling from the excessive heat – the grease was bursting everywhere, and a blob of boiling grease landed on my hand.

Unsuspecting and shocked, I jumped, knocking the entire pan of bacon to the ground – and the grease all over the open flame. A burst of raging flame covered the stovetop, and my brother began screaming in fear. His screaming was drowned out immediately by a blaring smoke alarm. The alarm finally woke Mom and V2 from slumber (V2 had replaced V1 as mate as V1 was in prison). I scrambled to scoop up the bacon as they both ran into the kitchen. I absent-mindedly touched the pan to my arm, causing a large section of skin on my forearm to get a 2nd-degree burn. Chaos ensued; I threw the pan as pain seared over my arm. I began waving my arm in pain. Both Mom and V2 were yelling and cursing, not understanding what an 8-year-old was doing trying to cook on the stove.

They tackled the situation extinguishing the grease fire and securing the pan. The immediate issue was controlled. The batteries were removed from the smoke alarm, V2 saw my burn and scolded me for being an idiot. He picked me up and threw me into the bathtub – turning on the water – the cold valve only. Mind you, this was wintertime in Illinois, as the cold tap water was COLD. He pulled the lever for the shower, and through my violent protest, he forced me to stay in the cold water for what felt like an eternity. Mom came in reacting to my screams and yelled at V2 to stop. He finally turned the water off, scoffing at her reaction, telling me that he was only trying to help and that this should serve as a lesson not to play with fire. I was sent to my room, still hungry and severely shaken by the entire event.

Returning to school the next day, I was forced to wear a long sleeve shirt to cover my burn. It wasn't abnormal for the time of the year, and I found myself wearing a long sleeve shirt everywhere until my burn healed.

SILVER LININGS

• • •

- It is important to be wary of attempting something you know nothing of. This does not mean not to adventure and pursue new things – simply to research and be aware of what you are going to do. You wouldn't fly a plane without having learned the basics, and you wouldn't cook bacon without having first used a toaster. This lesson has had some impact on my adventures through the years – most recently watching online training videos prior to renting a snowboard and attempting to make it down a mountain with zero experience. I had to ask three times for help boarding the lift... I left with a concussion.

Just Keep Swimming

I was summertime, school was out, the local playgrounds were full, and the pools were open. The pool was a treat we did not get to experience often, so when Mom offered to take us to go swimming – we jumped for joy. We got ourselves together and joined Mom in Grandma's car. Grandma had let Mom use her car to run errands for the day. The car ride was a little bit of a haul as the pool we went to was on the far side of town. My brother and I had not known until arriving, but Mom was not going to stay and go swimming with us.

Paying our admission, she left us with some cash for the concession. We weren't worried about it. We just wanted to get into the water! She promised that Grandma would be there to pick us up at the closing time as she left. We wandered off into the majestic concrete rectangle before us. It was a seriously awesome time; the pool had a diving board and a mounted hoop to play pool basketball.

We had a blast swimming with other children as we pretended to be basketball all-stars. My worries seemed to be a distant memory while there – no concerns about myself or my brother's well-being. We were truly regular children in those fleeting Moments. Between lifeguard checks (they make you exit the pool), we grabbed some nachos to split. The ones where they drench the tortilla chips in nacho cheese – they were sublime.

After some time passed, they announced over the speaker that the pool would be closing in 15 minutes. Heading to the locker room, we dried off and tossed on our t-shirts. We hung around a tall oak tree, waiting in the shade for our ride. We waited, and waited, and waited some more. Eventually, the parking lot was empty, and we began to panic slightly. A strange-looking man started walking towards us, and we took it upon ourselves to start heading in the opposite direction, towards home.

The sun was starting to go down as we began the nearly 7-mile trek back to the apartment. Today this is a normal jogging length, but at that age, navigating 7 miles of city blocks was a daunting pilgrimage. We walked the main road through town, Broadway Street. It was 80 blocks or so to get back to the apartment. After a dozen crosswalks and numerous silly conversations (what would you do with a million bucks? Buy a talking hamster, of course), we began to get hungry.

Counting our change, we had a few dollars left and opted to go into a nearby county market. I grabbed a bag of chips, water, and a snicker to split. When we rang it up at the cash register, we didn't have enough for it all, so I asked my brother to put back the candy bar. Continuing our walk home, about two blocks later, my little brother pulled out the snickers I had asked him to re-shelf.

It was immediately clear what had happened. We were both young and naive. I began to panic; I pictured us getting arrested and never seeing Mom again. Oh, crap, I thought, we are going to go to prison. I looked at my brother and went on a tangent about how we could end up in the place we went with Mom to visit V1. He began to cry, scared into submission by his big brothers' words and amplified by his already peaked level of adrenaline as a child pocketing a candy bar.

It wasn't until later in life that I understood he was genuinely trying to help our situation, and he took the bar out of love. (Seriously, my brother is the gentlest law-abiding individual I have ever known, truthfully it may have stemmed from this experience) A few Moments later, police sirens began wailing in the direction of our (over-dramatized) robbery. We both froze – I was convinced that they had been tasked to find the brutes that ransacked the county market. I told my brother to run, and we v-lined straight for an ally. We ditched our shirts (because they wouldn't recognize us with no shirts, right?) and threw away the perfectly good but criminally tainted candy bar.

We finished our journey about an hour later. We were walking through the door, in the dark, with no shirts, hungry and exhausted. Mom was at the kitchen table, drunk. She looked at us, and a glimpse of genuine shock came over her face. She jumped up, asking what had happened, where we went, and where our shirts were. She claimed she was going to have Grandma pick us up, but somewhere the communication to Grandma fell short. We ate dinner, we slept, and we forgave our Mom – because she was all we knew in the world, and we loved her.

SILVER LININGS

• • •

- All it takes is one genuine scare to change a person for life – my brother wouldn't steal a candy bar these days if his life depended on it.
- You can conquer anything if you keep moving forward.
- Do not enter a store hungry OR broke!

Don't Stay Up So Late

W e had recently relocated (against our will, due to an eviction), and I was attending my 3rd elementary school in the city. A few weeks in, I was required to sit with the school counselor due to a tardy problem. I was getting to school late, despite living near a bus pickup area. The counselor probed my life, asking about home, asking about Mom, Dad, and more. At the time, I was very well skilled in deflection. I made up stories and flew under the radar.

I explained that I had not heard my alarm on the days late and that Mom didn't hear hers either. The counselor advised me to get 8 hours of sleep and sent me back to class. The truth? I rode the city bus to school when I missed the school bus. Mom didn't have a car, and we lived a significant distance from the school. I missed the bus because I found myself oversleeping.

I overslept because Mom played music all night and continued on late-night benders with "friends." One night after my discussion with the counselor, I was significantly late to school. I had fallen asleep on the city bus, riding it around town three times before waking up and finally getting to school at lunchtime. I spoke with the counselor again and explained that it was my fault – I had fallen asleep on the city bus after missing the school bus.

I returned home after school to the Spanish inquisition from Mom. Why did she get a phone call that I was late for school? Why did I miss the bus? It does show up at the same time every day, after all. I didn't hold back and shared with her why I missed the bus. I couldn't sleep due to the late-night music and drinking. I was informed that her time was not an excuse for me to stay up late. That I could not miss school or be late and that this was very important. If I didn't and continued to be late, someone might come and take my brother and me away. The music did get quieter, and I did whatever was necessary to make school on time, not wanting to let Mom down.

SILVER LININGS

• • •

- Sleep is critical to performance. We need to be well-rested to maintain effort and focus throughout the day. If you miss sleep, you miss buses; you don't miss buses.
- Make the alarm louder or move it closer to your eardrums to ensure you wake up.
- Don't allow external distractions to impact your personal performance. If you must navigate loud noises in the night, sleep with earplugs – but don't blame the noise if you have options around it.

Dark Nights

About a year later, I was ten years old. Mom was experiencing serious drug abuse problems again. They had always been bad, but they were now controlling her entire existence. The abuse rose to a new level – she was abusing crack, meth, and drinking. More or less anything she could get her hands on. Moms' days were a blur of drug and alcohol-induced nothingness. She had not been in a steady relationship since V2 left her for a different woman to take advantage of (Mom's words, not mine). When V2 left, her capacity and ability to source drugs diminished significantly.

I recall witnessing numerous bouts of withdrawal, the results often terrifying. Sweating, writhing in pain, grinding teeth, crying, and puking. It was a horrific state. Mood swings were a norm for us. When Mom found her fix, she relaxed, escaping from her self-created hell for a handful of hours. These times brought my brother and me some solace.

One evening, we went over to one of Mom's "friends" so she could "visit." The true goal was to visit the drug dealer she knew that was most likely to give her something for nothing. Almost nothing. We traveled to a neighborhood worse than ours. (Difficult to pull off when you live in city-subsidized housing/projects) Walking into a house, there was an open hallway with stairs leading to one apartment with another on the main floor.

We traversed up the stairs, stepping over empty cigarette cartons, empty beer bottles, and what looked a lot like used toilet paper.

Knocking on the door, a guy came to the door, opened it, and grumbled something. I believe the grumble was to acknowledge that one of his regular "fiends," as he called Mom, had arrived. For the next half an hour, Mom tried to convince him to give her what I would call crack on credit. At the time, I did not completely understand the dynamics of the discussion. But ultimately, he gave her the drugs she wanted and mentioned he would be over later for payment.

As my brother and I drifted to sleep, someone knocked at the door. In a one-bedroom apartment, you hear everything. I peeked out the bedroom door to see the man we had visited earlier that day. They started talking, and Mom started sobbing. He told her to shut up and reminded her that this was what she wanted. A Moment later, he had ripped off her shirt and pushed her onto the couch. I opened the door and began to call out. The guy stopped, standing still as if he didn't know what to do. Mom screeched at me, telling me to close the door and go to bed – not to come out until it was morning.

I laid in the darkness, able to hear everything through the paper-thin walls. As she cried, I cried.

SILVER LININGS

• • •

- Do not ever expect to get something for nothing.

Darker Days

I could tell Mom did not want that to happen. I could tell that it broke something in her, something she really would never find again. The next day, Mom was quiet. She didn't get out of bed much. She had bruises on her arm, and her eyes were swollen and red. I had never seen Mom so distant, so quiet. I wanted to fix it, but I didn't know what to do.

I shared a CD with her I had gotten for my last birthday. On it was my favorite song at the time, "I'm blue" Eiffel 65. It seemed to cheer her up some, but it didn't change her state. The day after, an event occurred that would forever taint that song for me.

I came in from playing with the neighbor's child. I was hungry, but nothing was readily available, so I scooped up a mouthful of peanut butter and chugged some milk. I heard my song coming from the bathroom. "I'm blue.

Da ba dee da ba di" kept playing over and over. I loved the way the vocals sounded – I knocked on the door. Nothing. I knocked again and shouted through the door. I knew it was Mom because she had my favorite CD last. After a fruitless effort, I started getting anxious. I heard a knock on the front door; it was one of Mom's friends – a girl she had known since her teenage years.

She looked frightened, asking where Mom was. I told her she was in the bathroom and that I couldn't get in. She ran, pounding on the door, trying to get into the bathroom. She yelled at me to go get help – so I ran upstairs to get the neighbor. He came down to see what was going on, confused as to why a child was dragging him down into his neighbor's apartment. Moms' friend told the man it was an emergency and that she needed to get into the bathroom to save Mom.

She told us that she had gotten a call from her and that she sounded suicidal. The man kicked the door in and gasped. He ran over to the phone and dialed 911 as Moms' friend went into the bathroom. She began crying as she processed the scene. The neighbor giving information to the 911 operator, Mom's friend sobbing, I began to walk towards the bathroom. Moms' friend had cut the music and saw me approaching. She yelled for me to go outside and not to look.

But it was my Mom, I was worried, and it was too late. I looked into the bathroom. The floor was covered with pills, and blood was all over them. Mom was in the tub, incoherent, and she couldn't keep her head up – she was bleeding from both of her wrists. I started crying uncontrollably as the neighbor grabbed me and took me outside.

I didn't understand this experience any more than I understood others. I broke down, sobbing for my Mom. Why would she hurt herself? What did my brother or I do to make her do this? Police and paramedics came flying around the corner. Lights and sirens accompanied them all the way to our doorstep. Two paramedics rushed into the apartment with a police officer, and another officer stayed outside to question the neighbor and me.

My brother was with our Grandpa at the time, and I am grateful he didn't have to see this. Not too much later, the paramedics were carrying Mom to the ambulance. Her wrists were wrapped in gauze, and her body was wrapped in a medical blanket. The wrist wraps were soaked in crimson color. She was unconscious as she disappeared into the back of the ambulance. I thought I was going to lose my Mom forever. *

After the police wrapped up their questions, I was taken by an officer to my Grandpas. My brother and I didn't know how to handle this. We were children, and we continued to have what little stability we felt we had stolen from us. The phone rang, and Grandpa spoke to an employee at the hospital. Mom was going to be ok and would survive. However, she was being committed to the "8th floor", which served as the psych ward for the city. My brother and I would get abnormally acclimated to this floor, as Mom would end up there many more times over the years.

SILVER LININGS

• • •

- It's true that we don't often realize what we have until it's gone. It's a game-changer when we begin to cherish who and what we have in the present Moment – rather than reminisce their memory.

The 8th Floor

S tepping off the elevator, we were greeted by a large metal door with a call box below a camera. Grandma pushed the call button (Grandpa never visited Mom on the 8th floor, as he was usually the one working to get her committed there) and stated we were there to visit Mom. A buzzer sounded and the door opened for us. We found ourselves between two large metal doors. After the one behind us had securely latched, another buzzer sounded, and the door next unlatched for our entry.

A nurse greeted us and took us to sign in at the nurse's station. Passing several patients in bedrooms who had their door open – one yelled to us that the CIA was watching him. The CIA had bugged his popcorn and were listening to his thoughts. In another, an elderly man stood naked in the corner of his room, staring at the wall. After signing in, the nurse escorted us to the visitation room.

Walking in, there were a handful of circular tables with chairs—a couple of jigsaw puzzles in the corner of the room. The nurse went to find Mom – she entered; her wrists still wrapped from the self-inflicted injury. She looked like a zombie; I recognized the look – it was the same look she always had when suffering withdrawal. I knew she would be suffering by herself in the hospital without anyone or anything to help her through it. My heart bled for my Mom. We played Uno for a little while, Mom constantly apologizing for everything.

She made the same promise she always had made when she was in a bad situation – that she would never do drugs again. She would take care of us and put us first if God gave her one more chance. * And while I desperately wanted to believe it, I had begun to harden against the empty promises. As we were leaving, she began to cry at the table. Her wrists wrapped, her body drained; it all consumed me with pain.

The heartache followed me where I went. While staying with Grandpa, our supervision was not any more vigilant than it was with Mom. Getting to school on time and being home for bed was more or less the only requirements. I began failing in school. I even skipped a couple of days and ran around town. I had stopped caring, and I hardened myself against life so that nothing could hurt me the way this did.

I was spiraling out of control. I found out Mom was transferred to a state psych ward several hours away. She had been diagnosed with bipolar and schizophrenia disorder. This diagnosis later helped me better understand many of the experiences my brother and I witnessed in our childhood. At the time, it only made me think that I might be crazy – I googled the diseases and read an article that heredity may play a role in the disorders.

I was failing school and thinking I may end up on the 8th floor if I had similar disorders – then Dad called.

SILVER LININGS

• • •

- Sometimes we must accept that fact that others in our lives simply will not change. We must accept them for who they are, love them, but do not continue to put our emotions on the line in expectation of change.

Intervention

D ad called to check in on me. He had heard about what was going on with Mom. He knew I was failing school and skipping classes. He knew that if I continued this way, I would adopt it as a way of life. Not hesitating, he made the executive decision to have me move in within him.

I had always respected and looked up to my father – I also knew I needed to get away from Quincy. My brother was doing well, and he adored his life with Grandpa, ultimately choosing to stay in Quincy.

Quincy, IL Section 8 housing

It was a brisk Saturday morning when Dad pulled into the section-8 apartment complex. My bags were packed with what little I had at the time. All of it stuffed into a retro suitcase Grandpa had lent me. It was a rather unnoteworthy event, Dad pulled in, sat with us for a few Moments, and we were putting the suitcase in the car within minutes.

I said goodbyes to my brother and hopped into the car. Dad asked if I needed or wanted to say goodbye to anyone else. I didn't have anyone other than those I had already said goodbye to. I mentally said goodbye to Mom, the kids I knew, the drunks, the drug addicts, the bullies, but little did I know, I was simply trading one version of dysfunction for another. After a few hours of driving, we finally pulled onto Memory Lane (that's really the street name) and passing a couple of trailers. We arrived at Dad's cabin.

Oakley, IL Memory Lane

Dad lived with his wife and her two children from a previous marriage. They inhabited a cabin in the woods, only 75 feet from the Sangamon River near Decatur, IL. Dad was very much at home in the woods and on the river. A survivalist at heart, he would chop wood for winter, heating the house with an old-fashioned wood stove. He hunted for meat every year and always filled any hunting tags he had available. When he had time, he taught me numerous outdoor lessons. How to hunt, how to fish, how to shoot a bow, how to shoot a gun, he showed me several things from skinning a deer to filleting a fish – all things I had never experienced. *

Unfortunately, he was never able to shake the alcoholism. During almost all my memories with Dad, he was touting a natural light beer can in his hand. While he did drink each night, it wasn't the same as Mom's drinking. There were no parties, no late nights. He did not get violent but rather seemed more at peace when he drank. He never got loud, never got abusive physically nor mentally. He preferred grilling for the family over drinking with a stranger. He preferred a campfire and being alone to flashing lights and loud music.

Dad didn't force anything. He wasn't religious but felt content with what he had in life. He never complained and always worked with what he had available – and always worked for what he owned.

SILVER LININGS

• • •

- As children, we often only ever know what our parents permit us to experience. As an 11-year-old child, my world was held entirely within the city limits of Quincy, IL. I was limited to the trials of my mother and the day-to-day struggle. Moving to a rural area, learning more about the outdoors, and experiencing new experiences opened my world significantly.

A New Home

Soon after getting settled, I was introduced to my stepsiblings. S1 and S2 were good kids, and I sincerely believe in a different environment, we would have become a close family. Unfortunately, I came from a broken home, with an infamous nut for a Mom, and was overall no good. Or at least that was the general sentiment of my new stepmother. S.M. was not fond of the idea of raising a child that was not her own – and shared that feeling often.

The first week this dynamic revealed itself in our interactions. Talks were littered with "your dad" and "your son" and "my children" – all phrases that divided us from the starting line. Another layer upon this was finances. Dad didn't make a fortune and was raising a family of five on less than 25K a year. The stepsiblings had a father that made a high-level income and would buy them toys and clothes.

The division* began with the sentiment of S.M. and was enhanced with the division of material. Boarding the bus, it would look like we came from a different family on the lane – My Walmart shoes next to their brand-name outfits. But in all reality, we were kids, and had we been allowed to just be kids, everything would have been much better than it was. Because of the dynamic in which S.M. would put S1 and S2 on a pedestal – I was always envious.

I was envious because my Mom never protected me that way, and I was jealous because they seemed to have what I could not. They had nice new sneakers for the school year. They had the coolest backpack and other material items I wasn't given. * This became the new normal.

Dad was absent; when I would get up for school, he would be sleeping before starting his second shift job. He would leave around the time we were heading home from school and not return until almost midnight. Many nights I would fight to stay up in bed, waiting for his headlights to appear in the driveway – just so I could have 10 seconds with him as I ran out of the bedroom to get a hug and ran back to bed. It was something I looked forward to each day – because, during the day, it was her house, her rules, her kids.

SILVER LININGS

• • •

- It is critical to push for inclusion and balance within the world and especially within a household – by experiencing the rift that was created by words and intention – It is much easier to recognize and understand this dynamic with others. Always push for inclusion in all situations.
- When you compare your world to another's – you will always find something to be envious of somewhere. It wasn't until much later in life that I learned to stop comparing who I was in that Moment to who someone else was or what someone else had.

The Spatula

S M was an extremely authoritative homemaker – it was very much her way or the highway. I quickly caught onto this the first time I got into an argument with my step-siblings while S.M. was in earshot. In absolutely no way, shape, or form would this "unwanted" child harass her (self-perceived) all good, all-pure children. I had screamed at my older stepbrother, arguing about some cartoon on the television. In doing so, I felt a searing pain as S.M. gripped me by my ear and pulled me into the kitchen.

She tossed me to the ground with relative ease. This isn't difficult for someone four times your size to do. Scolding me, she brandished what had become the bane of my existence for some time – a large metal spoon. The kind of spoon you use to stir a pot of chili that feeds 20 people. She told me that anytime I did wrong, I would get beat – and she meant it. She slapped me on the ass with the spoon until I had welts. I crawled away, crying uncontrollably – not so much because it was extremely painful, but because I had never expected it. I was in shock at how quickly it had escalated to such a brutal punishment for screaming.

- It broke me, and I literally cried for my Mom. S.M. reminded me that I was there because she didn't want me – sending me to my room to think about my wrongdoing. I sat alone for the next few hours while my new family watched T.V. in the other room. I had never felt so alone in my life. At least I used to have my brother. As time passed, I wised up to the fact that she ruled the roost. I did everything in my power to avoid conflict*, at least in the early years. During this time, I always dreamt of escaping, of getting away, and while it would never happen, it was a nice dream.

SILVER LININGS

• • •

- I learned conflict resolution skills early on in my childhood. When you know, severe consequences await, it is fairly easy to actively avoid conflict.

Reunited

A year or so later, my brother came to join us and moved into Dads as well. I missed the crud out of him and was beyond happy to see him. In the same Moment, I realized that as happy as I was to be reunited with my brother, S.M. was equally disgusted with the idea of feeding for and caring for another child. Brother had packed on some serious weight. He had gained about 75 lbs. Since I had last saw him. He seemed less energetic than what I remembered – as if life had also knocked him down a couple of levels.

Grandpa could not continue watching him and decided it was best for him to move in with us. Honestly, I believe it boiled down to money – everything always seemed to boil down to money. Dad couldn't raise a house on 25K a year and still be able to send support for brother. It just wasn't sustainable.

Grandpa drove up to drop him off and visited for a little while. He cracked a joke about his weight, saying he was eating him out of house and home. I didn't care what the reason was; I was just happy to be with my brother again. But, as with most things in life, things change. * Our relationship was never really the same again after the time apart. I had changed, he had changed, and we wore both stuck in a whirling cyclone of dysfunction – just trying to get through it.

SILVER LININGS

● ● ●

- Change is an unrelenting fact of life. Among many others, our bodies change, our minds change, and our environment changes. We must learn to be agile and to adapt rather than resist.

Busted

I was sent to counseling with a middle-school counselor due to falling behind in some classes. During our discussions, the inevitable inquiry into home life came up. The counselor asked about my relationship with my stepfamily. I had been through enough similar interrogations that I knew to walk on eggshells. Despite this, during the course of our conversation – I mentioned the spatula and the beatings.

The counselor launched an entire investigation into our home and questioned all of the children. He brought in my stepmother and spoke with her about what I had mentioned. That night, I was given a "come to" speech regarding how hellish my life could "really be" if I continued to speak with the counselor about so-called "abuse." While nothing came of it – S.M. was frightened enough by the investigation that we never saw that metal spoon again. The punishment of choice became more psychological than physical.

SILVER LININGS

• • •

- Don't hesitate to stand up for yourself. There are others out there that are fighting for good every day – find them and reach out for help.

Everyone is Going to Prison

We found out through a call with Mom that Grandpa had been arrested for selling his pain medication. He was selling painkillers and was doing so with an unregistered pistol. What in the world was wrong with my family, I thought? Grandpa was the last one I had ever expected to go to prison. Was there more to him than I had ever realized? Who was the man selling narcotics while equipped with an illegally owned firearm?

Desc	Type	Date	Plea	Status
		12/21/2006		
OTHER AMT NARCOTIC SCHED I&II	Original		No Plea	Class 2 Felony
209 - Dismiss/State Motion		06/15/2007		
		12/21/2006		
OTHER AMT NARCOTIC SCHED I&II	Original		Guilty	Class 2 Felony
101 - Guilty		06/15/2007		
201 - DOC	3 years	08/09/2007		Concurrent
300 - Costs Only		08/09/2007		Concurrent
		12/21/2006		
OTHER AMT NARCOTIC SCHED I&II	Original		No Plea	Class 2 Felony
209 - Dismiss/State Motion		06/15/2007		
		12/21/2006		
FELON POS&USE WEAPON/FIREARM	Original		Guilty	Class 3 Felony
101 - Guilty		06/11/2007		
201 - DOC	4 years	08/09/2007		Concurrent
300 - Costs Only		08/09/2007		Concurrent
		12/21/2006		
FELON POSS/USE WEAPON/FIREARM	Original		Guilty	Class 3 Felony
101 - Guilty		06/11/2007		
201 - DOC	4 years	08/09/2007		Concurrent

Grandfathers' charges

During this same time, Mom had been in and out of psych wards. In and out of jail. This time she found herself with a longer sentence due to still being caught up in drugs.

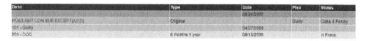

Desc	Type	Date	Plea	Status
		06/24/2007		
POSS AMT CON SUB EXCEPT(A/B/D)	Original		Guilty	Class 4 Felony
101 - Guilty		04/07/2009		
201 - DOC	6 months 1 year	08/19/2008		In Force

Mom sentenced to prison

With our family incarcerated, our summer visits to Quincy, IL, ceased for a time. * We weren't able to see anyone for a while. And while that wasn't a tragedy – it did lead to hectic summer visits.

SILVER LININGS

• • •

- Summer visits were something I had always looked forward to. I learned early in life (both from my personal experience and others) that incarceration not only impacts ourselves, but it also impacts others within our lives. Avoid at all costs not only for self, but for family.

Summers & The
Walk of Shame

D uring these years, the visitation had flipped. We would spend the majority of the year with Dad and visit Mom in the summertime. These visits were always exciting for us – getting to see family we had not seen all year and escape from the dictatorship of our stepmother.

Mom's situation never really changed through the years. Living on disability, she would jump from apartment to apartment from man to man, struggling with drug, alcohol, and mental hurdles. Nonetheless, we were always happy to spend time in Quincy for the summer.

Growing up in Quincy, I had an older cousin that I always looked up to. We had similar stories, single mothers trying to raise a child in a tough environment. Cousin was always doing something I thought was "cool," and I would try to tag along anytime I could. I often spent a large portion of my time in Quincy at his house. We would do things that many children do but would never admit to.

Things such as late-night "ding dong ditching" or "tee-peeing" a front yard. One summer, Cousin decided to take it to a new level. Suggesting a super soaker fight to be played in the front yard – we grabbed a couple of water guns to go. Disappearing for a few minutes, he returned with his gun full and a strange grin on his face. His apartment was on the second floor of the building. Heading downstairs, we headed outside.

As soon as I got down the stairs on the front porch, he jumped the gun and started spraying me. I wasn't surprised; that type of thing was typical. It wasn't until the spray hit my face and I inhaled that I was surprised. Urine – he had filled the huge super soaker with his own urine and was drenching me in it. I immediately began gagging and dry heaving – throwing my gun at him and running across the street.

Mom lived about 5 miles away at the time, and I traveled across town by foot, soaked in urine. I was partially sobbing as to why this would happen, partially gagging with each whiff of urine that caught my nose. That same summer, he shot me in the face intentionally with a B.B. gun, chipping my tooth – I didn't go back to my cousins for some time and never really looked at him the same after that. * This was devastating because, for the longest time, I thought he was my best friend.

SILVER LININGS

• • •

- It isn't until you have had a few "bad" friends that you know what a "good" friend consists of. Good friends listen, they care, and your relationship is supportive – not hostile or competitive.

Firecrackers and Silly String

Living in Illinois, it had never been a firework-friendly state. Quincy, however, was smack dab right on the Illinois and Missouri border. Crossing a bridge over the river, we could be in Missouri within a couple of minutes. It was normal for people in Quincy to travel across the bridge to buy gas, cigarettes, and of course, fireworks. The first few miles on the other side of the bridge were packed with gas stations, tobacco shops, and firework stands in the summertime. The craziest thing? There are no cities or towns nearby, the majority of the customers traveling from Quincy. Talk about smart business!

One summer, Mom took us across the bridge to buy fireworks. There was a backroad nearby on desolate farmland that people would drive to and set off fireworks. We grabbed firecrackers, roman candles, bottle rockets, and whatever we could get out of the "buy one get one" tubs until we hit our budget.

Making it to the firework road, Mom helped us organize the explosive materials. Splitting up the fireworks, she lit a punk (a punk is a term for "smoldering stick") for both my brother and me. We began playing with fountains, firecrackers, and the like. We were having a blast until a group of teenagers decided to intervene.

The teens were tossing firecrackers out from inside a jeep. One of the kids threw one right at my brother, and it exploded near his hand. He started crying as they sped off laughing. Mom looked at his hand and screamed at us to get into the van. She was having none of it. She only saw her children a handful of weeks a year, and these kids had just ruined her image of a good time.

In the van she had borrowed from Grandpa, she sped after the teenagers. She caught up to them on the bridge heading back into Quincy. Speeding every bit of 60 MPH, she drove door to door to the jeep. She was screaming at them and cursing their existence. They were visibly scared, shocked that something had actually come* out of their cruel joke. They tried to slow down, but Mom continued to match their speed.

She had bought a can of silly string from the fireworks tent – opening a can; she sprayed the passenger kid with it. They were calling her a psycho as they finally cleared the bridge and turned down another road. Mom contin-ued to curse the teenagers and that they had hurt her kid. My brother was in the back seat, more traumatized by the car chase across the bridge than the small burn on his hand. Oddly enough, that wasn't the only time that summer I would find myself speeding across the Stateline bridge.

SILVER LININGS

• • •

- Throughout my life, I have seen several instances where "karma" seems to catch up with individuals. In this situation, karma was instant and fierce. If you want good things to come from the universe, be a good person and give to others. Don't throw firecrackers at children.

Cosmo

M om introduced me to her latest and greatest mate. Cosmo was an interesting gentleman. The first time we met, I recall thinking to myself that he didn't seem like Mom's type. He weighed every bit of 100 lbs. soaking wet, was tall, and lanky enough to appear sickly. He was a heavy drinker and abused the same things Mom abused.

They dated and remained together for quite some time. During a visit, he was staying with Mom in her small one-bedroom apartment. With my brother at Grandpas, they had stayed up drinking. When Mom was drinking, she would smoke cigarettes at a rate that seemed inhuman.

She needed cigarettes, and as a result, Cosmo and I were tasked with a trip to West Quincy. (West Quincy is what Quincy's locals call the area across the Stateline bridge). I was bored watching basic late-night cable, and there's never anything remotely interesting on basic cable late at night. So, we made the trip to get cigarettes.

Regrettably, Cosmo had a little too much to drink that night and was not in a good state of mind. * I am convinced that he also battled mental issues because he had a strange habit of talking to himself. As we crossed into West

Quincy, he was having a full-fledged mumble-argument with himself. It was certainly a sight to see. Achieving our mission, we began the trek back across the bridge.

But way, way, way, way too fast. In a minivan, Cosmo's lead foot pushed the van to 90 MPH (after a decent acceleration period). And I found myself experiencing a miniature heart attack. He was laughing like a maniac the entire time. I was certain that at any Moment, he would take a sharp pull on the steering wheel and send us catapulting into the river.

As my cruel visions calmed, the vehicle slowed as we crossed back into Quincy. Getting out of the van, I ran inside (and told Mom what had happened) and cowered. Mom was livid, and at 2 AM, she was screaming and slugging on Cosmo. They were rolling around on the floor, fighting. He slugged her in the face – I ran at him pushing him off. I told him I would call the cops. He walked out, jumped into the van, and left.

Mom told me I wasn't calling anyone and that it was my fault he left. In her words, Cosmo wasn't fit enough to hurt anyone, and she had the situation under control. During their relationship, they would get into another bout, and she would stab him with a Kitchen knife. * No charges were filed – I am always assumed because it was true love.

HERALD-WHIG

Quincy woman arrested after stabbing

Police confiscated a seven and one-half inch kitchen knife for possible evidence in the case. Arrested was Fry, 32, on a charge of aggravated domestic battery. She was lodged in the Adams County Jail.

Local newspaper clipping

SILVER LININGS

• • •

- At all costs, avoid getting into a vehicle with someone you do not know or someone you do know if they have been drinking. Do your best to prevent them from driving for any reason.
- Do not assume your mother cannot handle herself.

Mercy or Merciless?

G rowing up at Dad's, we were in a relatively rural area, and there weren't many people to spend time with or things to do. Down the road, we had a neighbor that we had become buddies with. SB (stepbrother) and I would do all sorts of things with a buddy – jump on the trampoline, talk about girls, walk around the cornfield, and do other things that rural kids do. We had a pretty good rapport and would spend time at each other's houses – our parents were on short conversations and waving status.

Buddy was honestly more S.B.'s friend than mine, but I always tried to spend time with others whenever I could. One evening, Buddy came over to get us – saying his Mom needed help with a problem. As we are walking over, he explains that his dog has puppies. But there was something "wrong" with the puppies.

Arriving, his mother is half-hysterical, saying that the litter is deformed and that they need to be put down. Looking into the box of the litter of puppies was horrific. The poor puppies were squirming, half-developed. * Some were missing full limbs, and others, you could see their bones in some areas not covered fully by their skin.

Buddy took the pups outside, saying that "we" need to end their misery. He tells us to dig a hole for their burial site as he looked around for something to help him with his terrible task to end their torment. He was unable to find anything and, with little thought, asked for the shovel in the corner of his garage. He tossed the poor mangled pups into a garbage bag and then hard against the cement floor. * I had walked away, unable to stomach the entire scenario. I could hear him contacting the shovel over and over again with the cement floor.

The clanging finally stopped, and he picked up the bag, placing it into the burial hole in the ground. Tossing some dirt over them, we walked away as though nothing had happened. *

SILVER LININGS

• • •

- Life can be very unfair at times. What should have been a litter of beautiful little puppies reveal itself as pure suffering for the poor animals.
- Do not underestimate anyone – I wouldn't have thought buddy capable of crushing a soul. But, in his mind, he was saving them from torture. Good people can do terrible things when they are convinced it is for the great good.
- When you are faced with the decision to end suffering or permit a painful, unnecessary existence – how do you make that decision? You have to develop your own internal moral compass and follow it at all times.

Grandma Passes

Shortly after juggling the moral weight of the puppy incident, I got a call from Mom. It was a call from the prison; she was sobbing, telling me that Grandma had passed. * She had a tumor, and it was inoperable. Grandma was Mom's only consistent variable throughout her life. She was her grounding point through many of her life struggles.

She explained that she couldn't go to the funeral because of being incarcerated and begged that my brother and I attend. We had been somewhat close with grandma during our years living with Mom. Grandma always helped Mom clean up her messes. She would help with money and shelter when Mom had no one else. I told her we would try.

Dad was in earshot of the conversation and asked to talk to Mom. He asked who to call to get the information for the service and told her he would make sure we made it there. He was always trying to do right by family. The funeral was not that far out, and before we knew it, we were making the trip to Quincy for the wake.

Grandma had an open casket reception. It was the first funeral I had ever attended. It would be the last I attended for a decade. Walking into the funeral home, I recognized some family in the building. There was a short line of people waiting to see grandma and pay their respects.

As brother and I moved closer to the casket, I didn't know what to think. I had never seen a lifeless body and had many emotions cropping up as memories with grandma flooded my mind. Our turn to pay respect, an older woman walked up to my brother and me. She introduced herself as a friend of grandmas. She seemed pleasant, but there was something about her that felt off.

She offered to walk with us to see Grandma, and we made it to the casket. There was our grandmother, coated in makeup, looking as if she had lost 100 lbs since I had last seen her. The woman grabbed my hand without warning and put it on my grandma's. She held it there with force – I was confused and frightened. Not to mention horrified that I was touching a soulless body. Staring into my eyes, she told me that we all feel like someday, we all will die and be paraded for others to look at and judge.

I began tearing up, and a cousin of ours walked up to check on us. The lady let go and walked out of the funeral home. I never saw her again nor learned her name.

Wanda M. Wilcox

Quincy, Illinois

September 8, 1950 - September 9, 2008

Grandma

SILVER LININGS

• • •

- Death is something we must accept as a fact of life. This doesn't need to be a negative fact – rather, it should be used as a reason to relish and enjoy each Moment of life.

Open Doors and Dumb Kids

eturning home, I went on a walk with S.B. to visit buddy's house down the road. It was fall time and living in a wooded area; leaves littered the ground, barraging our vision with reds, oranges, and browns. It was the perfect weather, no overcast, a light breeze, comfortable t-shirt weather. Walking up to the door, we knocked to get someone's attention.

The door cracked open as if it had not been shut completely. We knocked again, calling our buddy's name. We felt we were close enough and had been welcomed in enough times to feel comfortable walking in. We walked around yelling names, but no one responded. No one was home, not even the dogs.

We putzed around for a bit until we saw Buddy's gaming system. Buddy had a gaming system similar to the one S.B.'s dad had bought him. Devious children we were, I 12, and S.B. a year older, we decided we would "borrow" a couple of games. We did, and I expected us to head home to play them. Naturally returning them later on – but, again, we were bored children. Buddy had shown us a gun his Mom owned in the past. We found that gun and took it with us and the games. We didn't really know a single thing about firearms at the time. In hindsight, the way it was handled was completely unsafe. We had no business taking it nor taking the games. Karma would remind us very swiftly that ignorance is no excuse and intentions do not matter in the court of law.

We hid the gun outside the house and went on to play games. The weekend passed, and we never even touched the gun nor really thought much about it. Heading to school Monday morning, the day began like any other school day. Breakfast, morning classes, lunch – I was called into the principal's office in the afternoon.

Walking into the office, I saw S.B. sitting in another room with a police officer. My dad was in the office with another officer, and I immediately knew that we were caught red-handed. In some sort of combination of Buddy's parents filing a report and contacting our parents asking about games and a gun – the games were found in plain sight.

The officers had no interest at all in the games. My heart was pounding, my pre-teen palms sweaty; I felt like my body had become a feather, and I would become unanchored and float away. * The conversation was short and to the point. The officer stated S.B. had informed them of the firearm location, and they had officers searching for it. The principal inquired as to what would happen with us. The officer stated despite the intention; we had committed a burglary that included firearms.

The firearms turned the crime into a situation that required we be detained for a hearing. Following confirmation that the weapon had been found, the officer gave me a Moment with dad and S.B. a Moment with his Mom before taking us to the station. We were both crying; we had never anticipated it going as far as it did. We were just going over to see our friend!

Dad calmed me and looked me in the eyes. He told me that no matter what happened, he would always help me and love me. * I stopped sobbing and hugged him. While I wanted nothing more than to go back in time and not have even gone over to Buddy's – we had done what we did, and there was no stopping all-knowing karma* from aligning our consequences with our actions.

SILVER LININGS

• • •

- True friends and family will be there for you through the roughest of times.
- It's pointless not to accept the consequences of your actions. This is a very stoic-like mindset, but it eliminates unnecessary suffering around variables you simply cannot change.
- Guilt is a universal feeling. Your body and mind give you a warning when you have or are doing something wrong. Sweaty palms and feeling light as a feather are signs – follow your intuition when it comes to navigating morality.

Wrapped in Chains

S B and I were marched from school in handcuffs. The officers took us to the police station to wait for the juvenile detention center officers to pick us up. Assigning our cells, we were told to hang tight. As we waited in our lone cells, each minute felt like an hour. There were no clocks, and the cells were isolated with a little window in the entry door that permitted a small view of the mostly empty hallway.

About 45 hours (minutes) later, we were buzzed from our cells and taken to a room at the end of the hall. We were placed in chairs and monitored by an officer as two large burly men wrapped in chains shuffled up the corridor. I had no idea what to expect. I was a 12-year-old kid that had never even seen the inside of a jail cell.

Not one from this perspective anyway – my cousin and I had been picked up for curfew in the past but sent home with parents by the time we made it back to the police station. This was different. I wouldn't be back in my own bed anytime soon.

The man threw the chains down on the table in front of us. He did not spare any dramatization whatsoever. He did not say anything to us, turning to the officer to confirm we were his pickup. Once he had all the information he needed – he radioed and another large man carrying chains approached. They told us to stand, our hands behind us.

They latched cuffs around our ankles and cuffed our wrists in front of us. The cuffs were extremely tight (on purpose, I'm sure), and the ankle cuffs linked to our hand-cuffs by way of another chain. We were made to waddle like penguins through the building and into a van with a "juvenile detention" sticker on the side.

During the ride, very little was said, and none of it in-cluded S.B. or me. S.B. was still emotionally scarred, with his face a pale red from tears chapping his cheeks. We were riding for about 45 minutes when the van pulled up to a barb-wired fence. We heard a buzz and the gate opened as the van moved forward into a garage. The garage door closed behind us, and we were led into the detention center.

Passing through several buzzing doors, we reached the receiving area. We had our mugshots taken, our fin-gerprints taken, we had to strip and put on detention gar-ments. We found out quickly that the naked squat and cough is indeed a real requirement for those being con-tained. We were put into another set of isolation cells as the center team decided where to place us. We were given a meal in our cells—some sort of goulash with a slice of bread, corn, and milk. In an isolation cell next to us, an-other kid was hitting his door and screaming obscenities. The correctional officers opened S.B., and I's cell after we finished eating.

Telling us to follow the single file to our new living

area – we began to walk across the facility. We passed numerous locked "pods" that housed other juvenile delinquents. As we came to our pod, we braced for impact. The officer opened the door, and we were giving a "grand tour" of our 20 by 20 recreational area, our assigned cells, and the shower area. The shower was as minimalistic as everything else. We were given a couple of squirts of soap and no washcloth with 3-5 minutes of water time. It was a rushed cleaning.

Finding our cells, the lights were turned off. I did my best not to get stuck in my head, but with four walls, no lights, and a small door window – it was very easy to become anxious. * The officers made their rounds every hour or so, checking on each cell. After a couple of checks, I finally fell asleep.

SILVER LININGS

• • •

- When you recognize that worry will only make your situation more difficult to bear, you tend to drop the worry.

Life in Juvie

B ecause a firearm was stolen in our fiasco, the law
required detainment until sentencing. On the 3rd
day in, we were taken back to the courthouse for a
hearing. In our jumpsuits, ankle cuffs bonded to handcuffs,
we were marched in front of a judge. Dad and S.M. were
in the room behind us on a bench. Our public defender
pleaded that we were first offending children and that I
wasn't even a teenager yet. The judge considered the de-
fendant's words and followed up with a swift decision.

The judge questions us briefly, seeking remorse – which
was plentiful in our current state. The judge questioned our
intention with taking the guns – we had no honest answer
to give the judge. The judge eventually came to the belief
that we were just arrogant and ignorant – both true. The
judge reminded me that had it been six months later in my
life, I could have been arraigned as an adult and given a
sentence that would haunt me my entire life.

Ultimately, the judge delayed sentencing, pending
a behavior report from the juvenile center in 30 days.
Essentially, we would spend a month confined, and the
correctional officer's report would more or less decide
our fate. S.M. gasped at the thought of her son being in

confinement for a month. The few days inside had already taken its toll on them both, and I felt genuinely terrible for S.B., who was taking the entire ordeal with extreme depression. * We weren't even given the opportunity to hug our parents and were taken back to the van. Back to the facility, back to our pod, and back to our cells.

SILVER LININGS

• • •

- Throughout this journey we take many of the little things for granted. Once lost, previously taken-for-granted items become strongly desired. I never realized how much I valued embracing family until I wasn't able to.

Best Behavior

The next day we were given a rundown of what our next month would entail. We would have school courses during the daytime. We would be given meals at the same time each day, and following lunch, there would be a brief recess allowed in which we were permitted "outdoors." The recess area was a small courtyard within the middle of the facility – it was an open concept (no roof) with enough room for a couple of basketball hoops. We would be given access to a "book trolly" once a week where we could get up to 3 books and swap them out the next week. On Sundays, a minister came. Once a day, there would be a pod meeting – everyone in the pod would be given an assignment or asked a question to share with the rest of the group.

If we behaved Monday through Friday, we were allowed to watch a film on Saturday. Needless to say, knowing my behavior was the variable deciding my freedom after the month – I was permitted to watch the movie every Saturday.

These thirty days taught me several life lessons that I sincerely believe I needed at the time. Without this experience, I am positive that I would have continued trekking through life without a care, without a mission, without deeper compassion for fellow human beings. Yes, I was concerned for my well-being. Yes, I wanted to be released and to see familiar faces. Yes, I was doing all I could to be the perfect inmate. However, through this journey of personal behavior correction, I found myself with a surreal understanding of other sufferings.

I found that no matter who we are on the outside, on the inside, we face the same emotions, we seek the same love, and often the same desire to feel important – to be someone. * In our pod was a young kid – he couldn't have been more than nine years old. Growing up in the "projects" of a modestly sized city, I was more than comfortable with friends of all shapes, sizes, and ethnicity. We became somewhat of friends during our time in the facility. During one of the group's sessions, he mentioned an experience where his Mom's boyfriend hit him. I instantly felt empathy for him. *

His father was not in the picture, and he was raised by a single mother. His mother getting arrested, he became a ward of the state. No 9-year-old knows how to handle that. He ran away from his foster home and snuck into someone's home looking for something to take and something to eat. Ultimately, he was assigned time in juvie because of the breaking and entering. We never met again after our time there – but one thing always stuck with me. He remained hopeful, despite the struggle. He was confident he would be back home with his Mom soon. I don't know where he is now, but I do truly hope he found his happiness.

SILVER LININGS

• • •

- We each face similar trials. We each strive for happiness. Being able to put yourself in another's shoes opens an entirely new perspective of the world.
- If the world was on fire, would we work together to put it out or still fight each other? It is so very important for our future generations that we conquer our perceived differences and unit for humanity.

Books

had never been one for reading at any point in my life prior to being put in juvie. During my time there, I became an addict. I was able to go on wonderful journeys of imagination each night in my cell. Under a very faint window light, I could read books for several hours until an officer would tap on the window and tell me to put it down.

I read Moby Dick, I read choose your own adventure books, and took every direction possible. I found a passion for reading while in that cell that followed me long after leaving. There was one book that literally changed my approach to life, the bible. I had never been religious, but Mom had always had a bible with her. She would take us to church on occasion, but it was never much more than a sermon or two here and there.

I was curious, and I found myself reading the entire Old Testament and many pages further. There was solace in reading through the construction of the ark (no idea what 300 cubits were at the time) and the turbulent times Moses spent in the wilderness. David downing a giant with his slingshot, the plagues, the commandments, and miraculous healings. During my time with the text, I absorbed many of the life lessons within – it was unlike anything I had ever experienced before. Using imagination to journey in the mind. *

SILVER LININGS

• • •

- Books can be a fantastic avenue for personal growth as well as an escape from the present Moment.

Freedom

I t was our sentencing day. As we were heading to the van, S.B. in tow, I revisited the last month in my mind. I had truly behaved like a saint in all interactions – only speaking when spoken to. I had become somewhat fit – picking up a habit of doing pushups each morning and each night. I found a serious passion for reading and an interest in theology. I was beyond confident that the sentencing would turn out in our favor. My confidence was supported – the judge, impressed with our reports, issued us three months house arrest, 200 hours community service, and 18 months' probation. * Following this, if we completed it, the charge would be dropped in its entirety.

SILVER LININGS

• • •

- Recognize that there are consequences for our actions. We should consider whether or not we are able to live with the consequence of the action BEFORE taking action.

House Arrest

School was just finishing for the summer, but prior to school finishing for the summer, S.B. and I were issued official expulsions from the public school we attended. We were criminals and would be an unacceptable nuisance to other students. The school feared for the safety of others as no one wanted gun thieves in their classrooms.

There was little we could do about the result – except accept fate and begin our summer of house arrest. * There was little to share from this time in my life – most days were spent in the same house, with the same people, and more often than not, the same routine.

┌─────────── SILVER LININGS ───────────┐

• • •

- There will be times in our lives in which we will be unable to influence the outcome of an experience. We must accept these experiences and continue moving forward. Live by the 3-foot rule – if it can't be touched (within 3 feet of our body) or we cannot influence it directly – accept that it is out of our control.

└───────────────────────────────────────┘

Milligan Academy

I t turned out that a 13-year-old child could not just stop attending school. The school referred us to "alternative" schools in the area. "Alternative" is a term used in place of "place of bad kids." We sent in an application for an alternative school called Milligan Academy. Dad and I went in and sat with the school headmaster, who inquired about our home life and lifestyle.

They already had all the information on what led us there – so there was little interrogation to that extent. The interview went smoothly, and we were given information about the school and a list of items needed to be in attendance. The school required uniforms that consisted of khakis and a blue polo shirt. These were to be worn every day with a pair of plain white sneakers with zero exceptions.

The idea was to create uniformity and inclusion among all of the children attending. Milligan was another perfectly placed experience that helped me develop as an adolescent. The school had daily morning meditation sessions in which the entire school (about 20 kids and five staff members) would meditate. Turning on a CD that emitted sounds of nature, we would close our eyes listening to crashing waves or chirping birds. I had never meditated until these experiences – mainly because I knew nothing about it. Nonetheless, this one simple daily experience became a staple in my life.

Milligan assisted with the completion of my community service requirement as well. For two hours each day, Monday through Friday after school, I would cross the street into a building that housed a non-for-profit community-based business. I would dump trash, vacuum, clean toilets, wash dishes, and other needs each visit. It wasn't fun work by any means as community service should not necessarily be fun – but it was fruitful.

I further ingrained my ability to serve others and would try to go above and beyond the call of duty when able. Rather than just stop after dumping trash, I would continue to wash windows. Rather than stop at windows, I would continue to mop the kitchen. I became a self-start, and it was beneficial – the people in the building loved my work, and the community service director who signed my hours would occasionally give me double the hours for my work ethic. *

SILVER LININGS

• • •

- Going above and beyond the call of duty is beneficial in all areas of life. Throughout the years, going the extra mile has led to many growth opportunities – especially in my career.
- I loved that Milligan Academy had a Phoenix as their logo. It is a valuable lesson – sometimes, you must let a piece of you die to be reborn. Let the past parish and be reborn in the future!

Milligan Academy
Providing Excellent Service and Programming

Better Behavior

M illigan Academy provided numerous self-growth experiences. During a couple of years there (age 13-15), I became a much more well-rounded individual. The school had tiered "levels" for students. Level 1-5 or something of that sort, with level 1 being the highest. With each "level-up," you receive new perks or rewards. Such as the ability to order out rather than have the typical school lunch tray.

There were also events that the higher levels would get to embark upon. Such as volunteering at the local zoo, soup kitchen, or dog shelter. Another well-designed event was the end of the year auction – each student earned "behavior money" that accumulated throughout the year. Each level received a certain allowance, and certain acts were rewarded with "money." The auction had all kinds of cool stuff, such as electronic gadgets, toys, and gift cards. Living with Dad, our typical household budget for Christmas was $150. (Divided between 4 kids). Naturally, I did everything I could to get as much loot as possible at each auction.

The catch? Levels and auction cash were designed to only be rewarded for good behavior. * Miss a day of school unexcused? Lose a level. Get into a fight? Lose two levels.

And just like anything worthwhile in life, the good stuff took much longer to gain compared to how quickly the bad stuff took it away. I worked diligently to gain level 1 and eventually did so. Earning my personalized polo with the school emblem and my name on it. I absolutely loved that polo.

But, just as with much in life, there are those who do not appreciate another's success story. Out of 15-20 kids in the school at any time, only 1-3 would make it to level 1. As such, oftentimes, rowdier kids would instigate with those on level 1 to cause issues. Remember, everyone in this "alternative" school had been expelled from public school. Some of them thrived on being the toughest in the school. At one point in time, a student jumped another student at the city bus stop after school with his friends. The next day, that same kid, after passing the required daily metal detector and pat-down, grabbed the other student and beat him until the teachers were able to pull him off.

The beaten student, face covered in blood, began to cry and ran to the bathroom. The other student went on a tangent and ripped off his shirt – revealing the atrocities those that attacked him the previous night had committed. I learned quickly to stay in my lane, be pleasant in interactions, and befriend as many students and teachers as possible.

Yet, I still found myself being ridiculed by the "tough kid." During lunch one afternoon, while I was eating chicken wings (level 1 was able to order out), a tough kid approached and sat down across from me. He started talking about how he had spent a year locked up for beating a grown man with a bat. He then followed up his story with an ask for a chicken wing.

I refused, informing him that it was against the rules. It had only been a few months ago that I was demoted for sharing food with another student. * The tough kid grabbed at my shirt and, missing the grapple, decided to clock me in the side of my head. It wasn't a super clog; he had to reach over the table – but it still strung. I learned a lesson that day. When someone instigates, it's worthwhile to think through a response. I had no idea that the kid would swing at me over a chicken wing. (Swing, wing, a rhyme! Ha) That day forward, I began to expect the unexpected.

SILVER LININGS

• • •

- The proper motivations can bring out the best in people. I desperately wanted to win some of the rewards at the auction, go to the zoo or any number of other things I didn't get to experience in my day-to-day life. It pushed me to chase reward, to work for reward, which has followed me through life. I have found that a strong work ethic and a willingness to go above and beyond coupled with diligent, focused effort leads to inevitable wins in life.

- Beware if you find yourself winning at life. The structure of win/lose is that there is always a loser. They may be sore and envious of your Porsche, career, or chicken wing. Do not flaunt your rewards, be human, and share what you can – sometimes, taking a hit to your reputation to lift another up is worth it. The student I had been demoted for sharing with previously was the first to stand up in my defense when the kid started swinging.

How to be a
Successful Criminal

O ne of my favorite self-growth experiences at Milligan was an after-school hours seminar with a man named Ron Glodoski. Ron was booked by the school to come in and give a speech to the children. Ron was a real-life thug who had spent some serious time in prison following a legitimate stint as a high-level drug dealer.

During the seminar, he said tons of things that connected with me, from an abusive childhood to seeking an escape from a troubled home. Ron shared a story of hope. It was a story of transformation, and it resonated deeply. * After witnessing Ron speaking with the class and reading through his book *How to Be a Successful Criminal: The Real Deal on Crime, Drugs, and Easy Money* by Ron Glodoski, Allen Fahden, and Judy Grant – I knew I wanted to do something similar with my life.

I wanted to transform myself. I desired to change my story. I wanted to drop the tunnel vision that so easily forms during those years. Ron left me a powerful message in the copy of his book I begged Dad to buy after the seminar.

I'm sure he wrote a similar message for several kids – nonetheless, this stuck with me for years.

SILVER LININGS

• • •

- When one realizes their ability to transform themselves, by themselves, the entire outlook on life shifts.

Message from Ron Glodoski

Milligan Graduation

Eventually, my time at Milligan had passed, and after two years, I was deemed capable of transition back into public schools. It was a bittersweet time; I had significant bonds with the staff at Milligan and had thoroughly enjoyed the school. There was a ceremony held at the end of the school year for students that either earned a diploma or completed the program standards. I retained a friendship with a couple of students. I even found infatuation with one of the girls, and we dated for a while. Interestingly enough, through her, I was introduced to my future wife.

My First Tattoo

Jumping the timeline back some, during my time at Milligan, I was dating Birdie. Our fling didn't last long, and we remained friends after our mutual breakup. Through Birdie, I met Fierce. I was 13, going on 14, and she was a year older than I. We had met briefly before, but it was during this time I realized we were attracted to each other.

S.B. and I were staying at S.B.'s friend's house. His friend's house was somewhat of a pig pen and was in the middle of Decatur, IL. The friend's father was present for our drop-off and did the song and dance speaking with S.M. She was unaware, but we had invited Birdie and her friend Fierce over to hang out. We all walked around town, SB, his friend, me, and the girls. S.B. was trying his hardest to get Fierce to date him, and it was becoming rather amusing.

As we walked through town, I found myself talking to and flirting with Fierce often. At the time, it was harmless fun. By the time their ride showed up to get them – I had Fierce's number, and we began texting regularly that night. That night I had another exciting adventure. The friend's uncle had just been released from prison (trust me, I don't know where these characters keep popping up from either) and was a "professional" tattoo artist. He also had a terrible crack addiction.

Half joking, I asked him for a tattoo. He didn't even hesitate and made a bargain with me. He said if I went down the street and asked to buy crack at the "trap house" (we were in a rough neighborhood) that he would give me a free tattoo. He handed me some cash and sent me up the street. The arrogant kid that I was, wanting to show them that I wasn't scared (and wanting a tattoo), I marched up the street.

I found the house and walked up to the door. I knocked, stood there for a Moment, and walked back to the house. It was (thankfully) a pretty lackluster trip. When I returned, he claimed he was watching me and that he saw me try. He then re-bargained and said that I had to "waddle up and down the block while quacking like a duck" to get my tattoo.

Easy! I did exactly that, and returning to the house; he handed me a book of designs to choose from. I picked a black widow spider – I'm not entirely sure why other than I thought it was "sweet." He asked me where to put the ink, and I told him my lower back so I could hide it from our parents.

Now, many of my life experiences easily mesh with the phrase "in hindsight." I am apologizing now for my over-use of this phrase. But, in hindsight, as a relatively stable-minded kid, I should have recognized that an ex-con willing to tattoo a 13-year-old kid was bad news. Nonetheless, we continued forward. The guy was smoking a crack pipe as he did the tattoo, and I caught it second hand. I didn't really feel much of the tattooing as I was fixated on a mirror resting in front of us.

I was lying down, the needle in my back, and I saw my dad holding the tattoo gun. * I vividly recall hallucinating from secondhand contact. I closed my eyes for the remainder of the tattoo.

The next morning after the tattoo, the friend's father came home shortly before SDM was due to pick us up. Friend had told him in private about the tattoo and drugs. He went ballistic. He began screaming, throwing things, and cursing at his brother, who had just illegally tattooed a minor. Calling him an idiot and myself a dumbass (I can't argue that point), he told his brother to get out. With his record and being on parole, he could go back to prison for tattooing a teenager in Illinois.

He ran off before S.M. showed up to pick us up – I never heard from him or S.B.'s friend again after that experience. S.B. and the friend made a pact not to tell our parents about the ink or drugs – knowing the seriousness of what had transpired over the weekend. S.B. wasn't one to protect me from any sort of trouble. But he could see the desperation in his friends' eyes, and they were close enough that he wouldn't share what had happened for well over a year.

At the time of the reveal, I was halfway out of the house. Things were anything but ideal, but I began spending as much time away from home as possible.

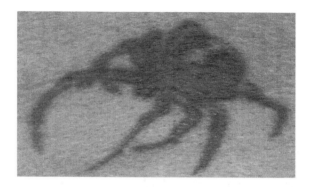

My first tattoo

SILVER LININGS

• • •

- Following this experience, I never allowed myself to be anywhere near someone potentially using hard drugs. I was convinced that the reason I saw Dad was because he would have been ashamed of my actions.

- All I had wanted for many years was his attention and approval, especially during the years that we had lived with Mom. Oddly enough, when he found out about the tattoo a year or so later – he had zero issues with it. * Rather than berate me, he shared stories behind some of the tattoos he had.

First Comes Love

During that summer, I spent a large chunk of my time messaging Fierce and finding creative ways to get together. For our first couple of months of "dating," we used her little brother as camouflage for our relationship. S.M. thought I was spending time with him as we were friends – but it was truly to spend time with her. Fierce's parents were also very "loose," and they had taken a strong liking to me. They often helped by picking me up and even brought her brother to meet S.M.

Dad was usually working off-shifts, so it was a while before he met them. Nonetheless, this worked for a while, but eventually, S.M. found out about our relationship. At that time, I was going to Fierce's house daily after school. Her Mom or dad would pick me up from school and take me back in the morning during the week. S.M. didn't care one bit in the end. She had never enjoyed my presence much anyhow.

S.M. and Fierce's Mom became "friends" and Fierce's Mom would navigate resistance from S.M. flawlessly. Playing double agent and effectively trying to be a "cool parent," she would even let Fierce, and I share a bed. We were also allowed to drink at home and more or less do what we felt like. * It was a difficult proposition to refuse – I was able to be with a girl I really liked and simultaneously stay away from S.M. During this time, I did regret drifting away from my brother and father, but I felt so much freedom that I buried those emotions.

During our early dating, Fierce's family took me on their vacations. Fierce had three siblings, two brothers, and a younger sister. Both of the sisters were competitive dancers – Fierce had retired from competition prior to our meeting each other. But her little sister was still in travel competitions. We went to Chicago, IL – to Davenport, IA, to Myrtle Beach, SC. I had never seen the ocean in my life!

I was awe-struck; their family had disposable income and lived a lifestyle that was outside my norm. * Fierce's Mom would even buy me clothes and other items. They ate out regularly and spent each penny available. It wasn't until many years later that I realized how dysfunctional it all was.

Fierce's Mom had an opiate addiction problem. She would permit us kids to have fun but expect obedience in return. During my time there, F.M. would regularly be drug-seeking. Hundreds of trips to emergency rooms far and wide, with invented alias, with imaginary ailments, in an effort to find those who would prescribe what was sought. At the time, these addictions seemed far less violent and life-consuming than others I had witnessed through the years. However, it took its toll as time progressed. * This monster would slowly siphon life from the family for years to come.

SILVER LININGS

• • •

- Experiencing a lifestyle above what I knew was intoxicating. It blinded me against many dysfunctional characteristics of our relationship. In the future I became more aware of such dynamics.
- All vices have consequences.

Drunk and Dumb (Kids)

F.M. had zero qualms when it came to utilizing the privilege of adulthood. From buying cigarettes to buying booze for minors – she did not conceive consequences in the slightest. I was 15 and would invite the occasional friend over for the weekend. During one of these such weekends, the group decided to take advantage of F.M.'s willingness to purchase alcohol.

I personally was never a fan of the taste nor the effects as much as others. F.M. entered a local County Market (good things never seem to happen when I am near these stores) with a couple of teenagers in tow. They walked through the liquor aisle together, and the kids were pointing at different liquors. As they pointed, F.M. would grab the item and put it into the cart. From the outside looking in, anyone in passing would have easily assume that she was purchasing alcohol for kids.

That evening, one of the kids staying overtook it to the next level. He chugged beers and, unbeknownst to me, chugged a significant amount of rum. An entire 5th bottle, to be exact (8 ounces short of a liter) of hard liquor. He could not have weighed much more than 100 lbs.

He was due home at the request of his parents later that night. We loaded up in the SUV to take him home.

I was in the back seat with him, sober myself, and kept repeating over and over that he was not okay and that we needed to do something. * He was unable to sit up straight and was slurring his speech so profoundly that everything he said sounded like gibberish.

I honestly had never seen someone so intoxicated in my life. We pulled over twice on the drive to his house for him to vomit – finally pulling up to his house, no one was home. Stumbling out of the vehicle, he claimed he would be alright. He continued to stumble up to his porch and into his house.

SILVER LININGS

• • •

- When we know something is wrong – we have a moral duty to act. If we do not take action, we must accept being a bystander and own the results.

Unnecessary Suffering

T he next day F.M. received a call from the kid's parent. They had found him passed out on the kitchen floor, dry heaving unconsciously. * Taking him to the hospital, he was committed to the intensive care unit. They were pumping his stomach and trying to reverse alcohol poisoning. I could feel the color drain from my skin – I had never imagined anything like this could happen.

Rushing to the hospital, we attempted to visit and check on him. I was able to briefly see him from a distance. He had an oxygen mask over his face and tubes protruding into his mouth; it was terrifying. My heart bled for his family, who had to see him in this state. I crawled away into a vending machine room.

Alone, one of his family members approached. A man, three times my size and twice my age, walked into the room. He had tears in his eyes and began pointing at me. Cursing, he said if the kid didn't come through this, he would rip my head off. I felt his pain and understood his emotions. I was sad, scared, and upset too. He turned and walked away back to the kid's bedside. We weren't welcome there, and without saying farewell, we left the hospital.

SILVER LININGS

• • •

Our actions impact many more than the immediately known. If more understood that decisions made impact others on a micro and macro level – perhaps outcomes would be different?

Investigation & Repercussions

I t wasn't much longer until police investigators were at the door. They questioned everyone in the house. F.M., Fierce, I, Fierce's siblings…it was nightmarish for everyone involved. But I have to imagine it didn't come close to the nightmare his family was navigating. F.M. reverently denied any knowledge that the kid was drinking. The investigators had brought a DVD with them and played it for us all to watch.

It was footage from inside the County Market store. F.M., and the kid, were walking together down the liquor aisle. As the kid points, she grabs the liquor and puts it in the cart. The officers pushed that if he didn't make it and she was proven guilty, she could be responsible for his death. Scrounging together a jigsaw puzzle of a story – F.M. advised the officers that he was helping her find items because she had visibility issues. Hitting a dead-end, the officers left.

After they left the house, the finger-pointing began. * This would never have happened if it weren't for me. Suppose it weren't for Fierce and me. It was our fault, and

F.M. was going to suffer for it. I admittedly felt guilty for all of it. For the kid in the ICU, for F.M. having purchased the liquor, and for the potential criminal charges. But none of that mattered much longer. I had gotten a phone call from a friend. The kid had regained consciousness and was recovering.

We rejoiced, but for different reasons. Happy that she didn't have to face any more threats of manslaughter, F.M. rejoiced. I rejoiced because life didn't perish needlessly, one that I felt I had put into jeopardy. The rejoicing was short-lived.

The investigators brought handcuffs this visit. The kid had given a statement that covered all basis of inclusion regarding F.M. He had picked out the liquor, he had drunk it with her permission, and every detail from start to stop. It was a terrifying and traumatic experience for her children. Watching their mother get handcuffed and placed in a police car. It was a terrible experience for us all – I felt their pain; memories of watching my own mother get taken away through the years flooded my mind.

I hung on to the words that it was all my fault. * The case would go to court. It was F.M.'s first serious criminal offense, and while the ordeal impacted all involved, the results were livable. F.M. would get sixty days jail time and probation. She was permitted to serve the jail sentence on weekends. Showing up Friday and leaving Sunday evening so she could still be a mother during the week. The family overlooked this and taking some ownership of the fiasco, I was forgiven, and my relationship with Fierce continued.

SILVER LININGS

• • •

- Beware of those whom are unwilling to accept personal responsibility. Be aware of situations in which we are unwilling to accept personal responsibility. Rarely are we completely guilt free.
- Later in life I realized that we can't take ownership for others action, only our own. To do otherwise is a fallacy that will only do us damage.

Life-Changing Moment

O ur relationship became much more serious without any warning. Fierce had been ill for a few days, and her Mom scheduled an appointment with her doctor. Following that appointment, I received a call, a Moment really, that would change the direction of my life forever. * Fierce called and asked me to meet them downstairs as they were close to home. She sounded off.

As she walked through the door, her head hung low. She and F.M. sat on the loveseat across from me. F.M. looked frazzled. Making eye contact with Fierce, she monotonously said, "you tell him, or I will." Fierce's eyes welled, and she turned to me, "I'm pregnant."

SILVER LININGS

• • •

- Our lives truly can be changed in a brief Moment. We should never underestimate the power of now and appreciate the weight that carries.

Ultimatum

F M looked into my soul that evening. She laid out the landscape very clearly. I had two options, we could get married and raise the child under her roof – or I was to have nothing further to do with their family or the child. I was in shock; I had no idea how to react. But I did know one thing. No matter what, no way, no how I would have nothing to do with a child of mine.

I made a decision then and there that I would do everything in my power to be there for my child. Reverently instilling the mindset that I would not let history repeat itself—knowing that the regular absence of a father leads to inevitable handicaps in life. *

We were in over our heads but Fierce and I did have a strong love for each other. While we were undoubtedly pushed forcefully to the path of marriage, it did not impact our relationship at the time. We were scared, unprepared, and unknowingly destined to fail, but we gave it a shot. F.M. did all of the logistical planning around the marriage. She even went so far as to help me obtain written consent from both of my parents – a requirement in the state of Illinois.

They questioned the integrity of the marriage but

ultimately stood behind my desire to do so. Fierce and I held our wedding five months prior to our daughter's birth. It was littered with bad omens from all directions. * The pastor who held our ceremony attempted to talk us out of it the day before the wedding. He explained that getting married for the sake of a child was a terrible idea. My Mom told me that I was too young to know what I was getting myself into. Yet, I didn't see it that way. I would have done anything to ensure my kid had my overwatch – the least of which was marriage. August of 2009, we were dubbed M.R. and MRS.

SILVER LININGS

• • •

- Having experienced early life without my Dad present, I knew I had to do my best to be present for my child.
- Sometimes bad omens may be worth consideration.

Downward Spiral

After the wedding, our relationship began to deteriorate. We were forced to grow up very quickly with little notice. We had stopped doing many of the carefree things our relationship had grown around. By the time our daughter emerged into the world – she was the only variable linking us together.

We raised our daughter for quite some time in Fierce's parents' home. Fierce loved our daughter, but she also despised the repetitive pattern and mundane day-to-day life. Understandably, no typical American 16-year-old "wants" to spend their days catering to an infant. F.M. stepped in often and helped with babysitting. I was in limbo, navigating between parenthood, Highschool, and the need to contribute financially to raising our child.

At age 16, I made the decision to drop from high school and start working full-time. I had my driver's license and two hands, and a child. I mainly did under-the-table jobs until I turned 18. Such as drywalling and construction work. From 16 forward, I really let my health fall apart.

I put on every bit of 200 pounds from age 15 to 18. I had tumbled into a depression and stopped taking care of myself. * I would eat fast food and adopt a cigarette smoking habit. At age 18, I weighed 350 lbs and was smoking a pack of cigarettes each day.

Overweight and unfit. 2011

My wife and I had given up on each other romantically – she had found a boyfriend who consumed most of her free time. I still kept the main thing the main thing, focusing on raising my daughter. That was at least until she wasn't around to focus on any longer. Out of nowhere, Fierce took our daughter and some of her items, moving into her boyfriend's home.

SILVER LININGS

• • •

- Interestingly enough, our bodies and minds seem to have a way of warning us that things are not well. When we become depressed, perhaps overeat, and cease having concern for ourselves – there is likely something that needs repaired or changed.

Estranged and Endangered

I was devastated, F.M. was blindsided, and the world I knew was turned upside overnight. I worried about my daughter every night she was gone – I knew nothing good about her current boyfriend. On social media, he touted gang signs and posted less than gentleman-like content. During this time, I decided it was best that I move out of the house as well. There was little keeping me there, and it was an uncomfortable situation.

I packed up and moved back to Dad's. He was more than happy to have me back. * He was recovering from his recent separation with S.M. They had split, and it was hard on him. He was convinced she had used him to raise her children – when they were raised, she ran.

Nonetheless, I was over the moon to be back with Dad. My brother had moved back into a trailer with Grandpa. It turns out that roughly translated into "playing World of Warcraft for living."* After a couple of weeks back home, I received a call from F.M. She had been on a video call with Fierce and shared horrific information. She claimed that Fierce had a bruise on her and that my daughter had a bruise on her face. She continued on to tell me that Fierce's boyfriend had said he would beat me down if I tried to come to his home.

I was upset and enraged with little more information aside from what F.M. shared. What kind of man puts his hands on a woman and child? I called Fierce and attempted to speak with her without gaining any ground. We spoke briefly, and she sounded alright, but I didn't get to see them or speak with my daughter. I was concerned and began working on the way to ensure she was okay.

F.M. was surprisingly helpful in this situation. She worked to get an afternoon scheduled with my daughter for herself. She informed me that because Fierce and I were legally married that I could take my daughter with me anywhere, lawfully. So, I did exactly that; during the afternoon visit, I met with F.M. to get my daughter. She looked alright overall, but she did have a slight blemish on her face.

Fastening her into the car seat, I began a four-hour pilgrimage from Rantoul, IL, to Quincy, IL. We would spend the next year or so there, in my grandfathers' trailer.

SILVER LININGS

• • •

- Somewhere, someone is available, willing, and happy to help us through a tough spot in our lives. Do not ever give up.

Grandpas Trailer

had spoken with my grandfather and ironed out the details prior to making the decision to take my daughter. It was bound to have a huge impact on her life, and I didn't make the call without considering the consequences. * Life at Grandpas trailer wasn't terrible, but it certainly was not glamorous.

In the trailer were my Grandpa, brother, our aunt, our cousin, my daughter, and myself. It was a single-wide unit, and my brother slept on the couch. My aunt had a child who was about the same age as my daughter. During our time there, they became very close. I hadn't stayed in the best of touch with family from Quincy. While it wasn't the best of situations to enjoy a small reunion – it was nice to be back with my brother.

SILVER LININGS

• • •

- Always consider all variables and potential consequences of actions. Again, if we are not willing to accept the consequences – recognize that before taking action.

Top: *Happiness is found in singlewides*
Bottom: *Grandpa, myself (middle), Brother (right)*

Order of Protection

The first thing I did after getting settled at the trailer was to apply for an emergency order of protection for us. With the bruising and the previous notion of violence from Fierce's boyfriend, I was not going to remain idle. I was also concerned that Fierce might get our daughter while I was working, leaving no lawful recourse for myself.

The judge rejected my emergency protection order request, reasonably stating that it wasn't fair, to not get more information from the other party involved. During the hearing, I was able to give a more in-depth explanation of the variables around the situation. The judge was much more concerned but still wanted to give Fierce the opportunity to defend herself. He postponed the case once more, and another hearing was scheduled.

Fierce came with an attorney to defend her case. But at this time, there was additional information from the plaintiff (Me). Fierce had just been released from jail prior to the hearing – her boyfriend also had an encounter with the law that supported my application for the order of protection. With the new information, the judge signed the 2-year protection order, which included visitation rights for Fierce that I had written in her favor. No parent should ever be withheld the right to see their child. *

I had experienced that while she was staying at her boyfriend's home. There's something about experiencing a specific type of suffering that makes you unwilling to inflict it on others. * It caused unrelated emotional pain, and I wouldn't wish it on my worst enemy. Despite this, despite having weekend rights, Fierce would not visit our daughter for the next couple of years. She decided to focus on her own life. During that time, she welcomed two more precious children into the world.

SILVER LININGS

• • •

- Empathy is something I believe all humans are capable of. In this case the Golden Rule plays a role – Do not do to others that which you would not have them do to you.

Trailer Life

The trailer was one of the worst units in the trailer part. It was falling apart both outside and within. There was insulation hanging out on the outside walls. Inside, the floor had holes in it, and it was stripped down to the plywood. It was not the most sanitary living – with Grandpa owning a dog – the dog was not house trained properly. I often find myself cleaning the trailer even as the only one in the unit with a job.

The trailer itself cost Grandpa a little less than $3,000, and he paid $150 a month in lot rent. My daughter and I lived in the trailer for a little over a year. While living there, Grandpa charged us $300 a month in "rent." I didn't mind because I was simply happy to have a roof over my head * – we had a 10 foot by 10-foot room that my daughter and I shared. It was a tight fit, but I never once complained, even as the only one in the trailer paying "rent." Over time there not only did I cover the lot rent, but I also imagine I likely paid the unit purchase price in full.

SILVER LININGS

• • •

- Things may get bad, but no matter how bad they get, we can always find something to be grateful for. If nothing else, gratitude for the ability to simply experience experiences. (it's deeper than it sounds!)
- We must additionally recognize that on a plant of seven billion – someone, somewhere is struggling more. We must pick ourselves up so we can find them and help lift them up.

Life Lessons as a D.S.P.

While living in Quincy, this go around, I was 18, and I had just earned my G.E.D. Grandpa had a friend (whom I later found out he was selling drugs to) who worked at a local care center for individuals with learning disabilities. These were centers where either the state or families funded the center to care for disabled adults.

She set me up with an interview for a D.S.P. role. A DSP is also known as "direct service personnel." In its simplest form, it is a C.N.A. without the certification. I personally didn't mind what the work was – I was eager to get to work and have funds. Looking forward to purchasing my daughter and I much needed items. On a side note, I will admit that my daughter and I were getting food stamps and Medicare during this time. I never enjoyed being on welfare, but I am immensely grateful for a government that provides this for those in need. It truly made a colossal difference in sustaining our lifestyle (survival in general).

I did great during the interview, and the position was offered to me the following day. Their team was excited to get an extra pair of hands-on site. Within a week of the background, drug screen, and required T.B. test, I began my first day as a D.S.P.!

Having experienced a healthcare role firsthand, I can wholeheartedly say that those that work within the field are superheroes. I learned so many valuable life lessons during my relatively short time as a D.S.P. that it is hard to express my overwhelming gratitude for the experience.

During my first day on-site, I was introduced to a myriad of awesome individuals. The center I worked in had less than ten beds – so I was able to bond with many of those there. One gentleman, R, was blind and had the mental level of a 9-year-old. R was in the normal retirement age range for our society – but always behaved like it was recess time in 2nd grade. He had a wild spark for life. Every day and everything was an adventure for him. He would get giddy while listening to baseball on the radio – with zero cares as to who was playing or winning. R may have held the form of a grandfather, but he chirped with the spirit and imagination of a creative child. *

R was the only resident in the center able to speak coherently. M, another older gentleman, had the mental capacity of a 2-year-old. He understood emotions, gestures, his name, but little else. One of his intense characteristics was his immeasurable energy. Imagine a man in his 60s, rolling around, giggling, picking his nose, and not having a single care in the world – that's M.

Others in the house were wheelchair or bedridden due to their physical and mental limitations they struggled with from birth. * As a D.S.P., my job was to dress, bathe, feed, entertain, do laundry, and monitor the residents. There were usually a couple of D.S.P.s at the house in addition to an R.N. to issue medication when needed. So, the life lessons, you ask?

While working in the home, I was first and foremost humbled. Many there had never been given the gift of mobility or the ability to learn, read, or even speak. All things I had taken for granted every day of my life. I very quickly had a newfound appreciation for the basic functions and senses I am able to enjoy every day. Running, reading, singing, smelling, comprehending, dancing, and more all mean so much more when you truly imagine life without them.

I found an empathetic muscle I had never used much prior to being a D.S.P. Others tackle so much more than we will ever know on the outside looking in. I learned to never ever judge a book by its cover. I repeatedly learned the importance of patience. There is simply no wrestling a grown man into clothes if he isn't ready to wake up.

You CANNOT change a full diaper while the one being changed is attempting to do the worm. You never take a sunset from someone who is engulfed in it. You simply sit, take a deep breath, and slow down the area in your mind that pushes you to always be moving. *

I learned to appreciate the little things. R was a huge proponent of bringing out the child within me, and I still thank him often in thought for that priceless gift. R would get so excited about the little things, a walk outside, a song on the radio, the warm sun on his face. Despite being blind, R had the most intense facial expressions, the largest smiles, and a true chirp of gratitude for life came out in his words. R once gifted me a small toy soldier. He was so happy to surprise me with it – I naturally expressed overwhelming appreciation. I keep the toy soldier on my office desk as a regular reminder – don't lose your inner child, your imagination, your sense of adventure!

Always keep that piece of you with you, and all things – everything little thing – can be gigantic. R's catchphrase has been a staple in my life ever since I left the center. "I'm just happy to be here" *.

Courtesy of R

SILVER LININGS

• • •

- Don't judge a book by its cover. We often have the habit (or at least I have) of judging events or people based on our personal bias. We don't truly know what is going on under the social mask that others wear, and it is never safe to assume.

- Be patient! If you don't slow down to smell the flowers occasionally, you might just get some poop on you.

- Stay grateful, appreciate your senses, appreciate the little things – the fact that you can read these words is a true miracle! Never forget that others are brought into and take out of this world without even being given the opportunity to appreciate those things we take for granted.

- Keep a piece of your inner child with you always.

Upward and Onward

While I loved working at the home – I was unable to financially make ends meet there. Working minimum wage ($8.25/hr. at the time) and less than full-time was not survivable. My average weekly take-home there was around $200/week after taxes. Bidding farewell to my friends at the home, I moved into a career path. I had landed a position as a tire and lube technician at Walmart's tire center.

Following several onboarding videos, I was introduced to my new coworkers. They were an interesting bunch (if you have ever worked at a supercenter – everyone is interesting), saying the least. Yet, I still got along with each of them. * While at Walmart, I learned a valuable lesson regarding failure.

SILVER LININGS

• • •

- Being a friendly person and befriending others has been a staple for me in my career growth. Strong working relationships and professional networking will lead to numerous opportunities.

Flat Tire

The learning curve was more like a learning cliff at Walmart. I was thrown in with zero training outside of safety videos (interestingly enough, sink or swim became a pattern through my career). My first task? A flat tire repair on a little beetle car. I was eager to prove myself – I pulled it in, put it on the lift, and took the wheel off from the vehicle. I had seen others do it and was following the steps I was given. "Pull the car in, take the tire off, put it in the dip tank" it was pretty straightforward.

I used the tire machine to pull the tire off of the rim. I took the tire to the dip tank, which was used to find leaks; the idea was to dip the tire into the tank and find the leak through the visual of bubbles of air escaping from the tire. I couldn't find the air leak and asked a coworker for assistance.

My coworker came over and looked at the tire. He looked at me, and he looked at the tire – looking back at me, he burst into laughter and began calling for the service manager. The manager came over, and through gasps of air and tears, my coworker pointed at the tire, the dip tank, and at me.

The manager apparently immediately picked up the

joke I was missing. Collecting himself, the manager explained to me in as pleasant a manner as possible – the tire needed to be on the rim, with air in it, to find the leak. I had a eureka Moment and couldn't believe what I was doing. I had removed the rubber from the rim and was twirling a tire with no air inflation around in the dip tank.

I burst out into laughter myself and thanked them as I went back to the tire machine to remount the tire. The lesson I learned here was twofold. Always learn from your mistakes* (I assure you I never made this mistake again), and do not hesitate to laugh at yourself.

SILVER LININGS

• • •

- The ability to accept criticism with a growth mindset and to truly learn from mistakes is priceless.

Time to Move on

I spent the next stint I lived at Grandpas working at Walmart. I thoroughly enjoyed working in the shop. It's difficult to find that shop smell elsewhere. There are not many places that smell like warm oil and burnt rubber. Had external factors not pushed me away from Quincy – it is difficult to say how long I might have worked in that role. I had become comfortable with the day today. But more and more events cropped up that made me wake up to the need to leave the city.

Mom had been sent to the department of corrections for another drug charge. Grandpa was making a living selling pain medication that was prescribed to him—suffering through physical pain in exchange for the little amount of "freedom" that cash offered. I had no friends at the time. One acquaintance that I worked with at Walmart quit the job soon after I lent him my G.P.S. and never returned it. My daughter wasn't happy and was often bickering with her cousin due to being cramped in the trailer. My brother was stagnating, spending his days in front of an LCD screen. I knew deep down if we did not get away from that city, our lives would be consumed the same way I had seen it consume others. *

I made a judgment call to move back to the area our dad raised us in. We moved from the trailer in Quincy into a trailer on Memory Lane. It was extremely cost-effective. The trailer lot rent was only $800 a year, and the unit itself was practically free. It was on the river, and water was pulled from an underground well. Me, my brother, and my daughter settled into life on Memory Lane fairly well.

SILVER LININGS

• • •

- At a previous time in my life, I had not heeded "bad omens". When the universe starts inserting red flags into our lives, we must pay attention.

Interestingly enough – we never had satellite services.

The Straw that Broke My Back

As we moved into the trailer, it seemed everyone elsewhere was falling apart. F.M. had been sent to prison, Mom was in prison, and Grandpa was also sentenced to prison for selling his medication. Luckily, we had seen the writing on the wall in Quincy, and I was grateful we acted on it. It was time to focus on ourselves, and we needed a life change. I needed a life change.

I had put on an extreme amount of weight over the last few years. I weighed more than 350 pounds. I was a single parent. A high school dropout that barely had earned his G.E.D. I was broke and living check to check in a trailer. I had no goals and no plan. We traveled to food pantries to keep food on the table. We would scrounge for change to go to the laundromat. We didn't have our own vehicle. I felt like a failure – I felt that I was failing my daughter.

I refused to fail my daughter. I made a promise in that trailer that I would do whatever it took to improve myself and elevate my family. * The next year was one of the toughest uphill battles I had ever faced.

SILVER LININGS

• • •

- There may be times in our lives in which we feel suffocated by our life results. I have heard some call it a mid-life crisis. I have heard others call it a mental breakdown. When we reach that point, we have two options, give in or fight forward.

Trailer Transformation

started then and there to turn my life around. I wasn't sure where to start – so I began with what I knew. * I searched YouTube for things such as "how to improve my life" and "how to earn more money." I found a wealth of material on YouTube that penetrated my soul – oddly as that may sound. I found Tony Robbins, Jim Rohn, Les Brown, Wayne Dyer, Bob Proctor, Zig Ziglar, Brian Tracy, John Maxwell, and so many more individuals that shared methods, strategies, and pathways to improve my life. I was at a point in my life where I was ready to fight for change.

I stopped blaming others and took ownership for my life. * I picked up sayings such as "For things to change, you have to change" from Jim Rohn. We are not trees, and we do not have to stay in one place. We are not ducks, and we do not have to fly south. We get to choose our own path – no one else decides for us. Things that are easy to do – are also easy not to do. It all depends on our discipline, motivation, and goals. After all, without goals, the next ten years are going to be a lot like the last ten years – I was not about to let that happen.

I listened to all that was available daily. Tony Robbins from a struggling home to a powerhouse businessman that helps others selflessly. Wayne Dyer, from the struggles of a foster home to a respected educator and world renown author that helped millions – including myself. Les Brown, also navigating a tough childhood, chose to transform himself into a world-class public speaker. Brian Tracy, from low-level labor roles to best-selling author. Bob Proctor, janitor to millionaire. Zig Ziglar, from suffering sales to sales master.

The names varied, the styles varied, but the message to me was universal. Anyone from anywhere can change their external environment if they work to change their internal environment. I understood that at a very surreal level. I got a library card and began reading nonfiction and technical books – for free! I followed the advice of several of these giants and used my free time to listen to audiobooks and learn.

I began doing fitness videos from YouTube and eating healthier. I was riding a bicycle everywhere I went and stretching regularly. I did everything in my personal power to begin building myself up day by day. Soon, things began looking up. I landed a position at a local sears store as an automotive tech. I was working full-time and learned much while there. I learned how to do alignments, brakes, alternators, and more – I even purchased a large toolbox.

I took a leap * and applied to community college. I initially failed to test into college-level courses and was told to try again after "brushing up" on my skills. I began a personal regimen of math and English studies. I went to the library and requested workbooks that I would make copies of. I completed several basic math study guides cover to cover. My next attempt at the testing – I qualified for entry-level college courses. With the help of the Pell grant, I was able to start college studies. I started slow, working full-time and raising my daughter. I didn't want to overwhelm myself. Before I knew it, I was a full-time student in addition to a full-time father and employee.

The positivity of the mentors I found within the videos, books, and audiobooks all compounded into what I can only define as personal happiness. I was making and chasing progress. As Tony Robbins says, "Progress equals happiness." I became and have been since a "self-improvement weirdo." The guy that gets weird looks from the normal people. Ever since this change of mindset in my life I approached the day to day differently. I would jog with steel toe boots on during my lunch break in wintertime. I turned down nights and weekends out in favor of study. Instead of blasting music in the car, I blasted audiobooks.

I removed sugar from my diet entirely for more than a year. I took my physical training more seriously and started going to the gym regularly. Physical activity became a source of stress relief rather than a source of stress. But, despite all of my internally focused growth, the external world still lobbed curveballs.

SILVER LININGS

• • •

- I have that knowing where to start is not as important as simply starting.
- Personal ownership of ALL of our life results is one of the first barriers to true self-transformation.
- Failures are an inevitable precursor to success. Do not be a perfectionist, be a failure conqueror!

I navigated from being unable to jog a block to running marathons.

Sears Closes

was in my 3rd semester working on a criminal justice degree when I found out. The store was closing, along with many other stores across the nation. It was a devastating blow for me, but much more so for others. Store management called a store huddle and pulled everyone on shift that morning together. In a monotone voice, with zero emotion, warning, or even an attempt to soften the news – "Our store will be ceasing operations this October."

The manager, through the tears of employees, continued on to inform the team of the closing plan. A staged "everything must go" sale in which the store would offer increasing discounts as the closing date moved closer. Nothing regarding appreciation for the years of service, nothing about the effort of the employees, zero words for those impacted. * The entire store was issued its termination with no warning and no humanity. I felt so terrible for the others there – would they be alright? Surely, they had families just as I did to support them.

I vowed to have a new job lined up before the store closed. It was July, so thankfully, they gave everyone ample time to job search. One coworker suggested I visit a company that hired companies needing assistance. Within two weeks of going to this hiring company, they had offered me three different jobs. I turned down two and jumped at the third – one that would expand my current skillset – a diesel mechanic position.

SILVER LININGS

• • •

- When accepting the responsibility of leadership, it is critical to be willing to help those you lead navigate bumpy terrain. Watching this leader break numerous colleagues' hearts without any apparent concern for the team impacted me significantly.

Mack Trucks

T he first day on the job should have been filled with reds flags, from the cursing coworkers to the lack of smiles and the shunning of the new guys that had arrived. But again, at this time, I was a certified weirdo. I was far too engulfed in enjoying life than to spare time concerned for negativity. * I dropped off my tools, got organized, and reported for duty 30 minutes early.

I was given menial tasks at first – such as cleaning the floors or helping other mechanics clean up their bays. I am unsure if it was to gauge my ability or to gauge how thick my skin was – either way, "I was just happy to be here".

As time passed, I learned an enormous amount about the trucking industry and diesel tractors themselves. From full frame rebuilds to engine overhauls and electrical diagnostics, I was enthralled. I was convinced being a diesel technical was my destiny. I trained for and earned several automotive service excellence certifications (A.S.E.) for diesel repairs.

I transferred into a diesel program at community college and brought the extra dealership hands from students seeking a career in my classes. Over the time there, I invested several arms and legs into my tools – I worked with the technician program teacher and got the dealership invited to a radio interview around hiring aspiring technicians through the community college. But, as there always seemed to be, someone was ready to try and knock me down a level or two.

Students learning to keeping trucks rolling

Chris Lusvardi   Dec 6, 2015   0

Jake Fry check the diagnostics while working with Jason Jeros at Decatur Mack.
Herald & Review, Lisa Morrison

Working in the shop, myself on the right.
Herald & Review, Lisa Morrison

SILVER LININGS

● ● ●

- When I began my internal growth journey, external negativity did not stand a chance.

The Shop Bully

During my time in the shop, I learned as much about social behavior as I did about diesel mechanics. It was a tough lot in the shop! And if I had not been a little "high on life," I am not so sure I would have made it with them. Despite being ridiculed often for being the new guy or even the least experienced for quite some time – I would still buy the team Saturday breakfast and hand out Christmas cards.

Yet, there was one gentleman who always had something negative to say or had a hurtful joke ready to fly off his lips with zero contemplation. * Again, it was a rougher-than-normal work atmosphere, and a daily cursing count of 100+ was the norm. It was labor-intensive on often filthy equipment (consider crawling around under a trash truck as maggots fall onto your face) with stressful unknown variables. Oh no, you just snapped a head bolt. Have fun drilling for an hour while being heckled.

Nonetheless, I was making a couple of dollars more an hour than I was used to. As I mentioned, I would use what I considered extra income to bring in the occasional batch of donuts or McDonald's buffet. There is something about being the lowest on the "social totem pole" and bringing smiles and gifts that people just simply do not know how to respond to. * A few months of this and the bullying turned into a "talking shop."

As time continued to pass, I continued to invest in my career as a diesel technician. I joined Mack's manufacturer technician training course and earned a dealership certification. I then set my eyes on the trucking industry's holy grail – a commercial driver's license. I saved up for nearly a year to pay for the CDL course at the community college. It cost nearly $4,000 to attend and had to be paid in advance.

SILVER LININGS

• • •

- We must learn to navigate all types of personalities in the world. Many will be positive, but some will inevitably be negative. Learn to overwhelm the negative with positivity. Be the change you want to see – responding with like will lead to like.
- Kill them with kindness – I have always found a true smile and compassion for others to nullify and render useless others negative intentions with time.

CDL Class

invested my savings into the night CDL course at the college. * For two months, Monday through Friday, after a 10-hour shift, I would spend 4 hours learning how to drive a tractor with a 53-foot trailer. I was blessed in several forms in the night course. As the only student (who wants to work on themselves from 5-9 PM? M.E.!) I had the entire 4 hours to myself to learn how to drive.

I, the truck, and the instructor who was nothing short of an awesome instructor. He was a retired compliance manager for the private fleet of a large agribusiness well-known in the area. Archer Daniel Midland (A.D.M.). He shared stories of his career and the value that truck drivers bring to the country. He was a trucker himself through and through, starting his career transporting goods for a potato chip company "back in the day."

I learned many strong lessons from him – one of the gems being the value of being a good person and working with integrity. He had worked his entire life as a hard worker, a laborer, a driver, and eventually a manager. He was evidence that a man who works hard and takes care of his family wins in the end. He was a staple in the community helping aspiring drivers learn how to navigate a commercial vehicle. He had retired with a boon of stock from A.D.M. and had enjoyed his job so much he didn't even know they offered a pension until he retired! Talk about a good gift for a good person.

Being one on one every weekday for two months, our rapport grew significantly – eventually, he suggested I consider working for A.D.M. At the time of the suggestion, I couldn't vision myself anywhere back at the Mack dealership. But as time passed, a career change began to make more and more sense. A.D.M. offered a 401k, a pension, health, dental, and vision insurance in addition to numerous other benefits I had never had in my past. The financial aspect of the comparison was a no-brainer, but would I do with my tools? My schooling? I shelved the consideration for a while.

SILVER LININGS

• • •

- Use earnings to invest in self often. The knowledge and skills learned from these experiences that require investment will often open up more doors in the future. I have also found that those items we spend our funds on are given more attention than those we do not.

Pushed in a New Direction

N ot too long after earning my CDL, I approached the dealership manager to attempt to negotiate a pay raise. After all, a CDL was an important skill at a commercial vehicle dealership. But, as it turned out, it wasn't an important skill at this dealership. Not only did I not receive a raise – I had more jokes hurled at me. Here comes "Big rigger Jake"! * This pushed me to realize that I had already hit my glass ceiling at the shop.

I applied with A.D.M. and was hired within a couple of weeks of submitting the application. Within the next month, I had insurances, a retirement plan, and was making double the annual wage I was making as a mechanic – talk about a level up! *

SILVER LININGS

• • •

- Know your worth, and do not ever let anyone decide your worth for you. If your skill sets have elevated, you into being prepared for a higher paying role or made you worth more to the market – chase every penny you deserve. After accepting my worth and pivoting my career, I doubled my income in a couple of weeks.

- Invest in yourself! The $4,000 I invested in earning a new skill (CDL) has brought me priceless returns through the years. I still hold my CDL as a valuable skill that will always be able to put food on the table.

Climbing the Corporate Ladder

joined A.D.M. as a truck driver in 2016. It was a brand-new adventure, and I was beyond excited! The drivers at the terminal are union, and that was also a new experience. I spent a couple of months training with a professional driver trainer. As I had no experience driving outside of around the lot at Mack – I had some serious learning to do. The trucking location hauled primarily liquid bulk shipments. From oil and sweetener to hazardous acid (the kind that eats flesh), we delivered all over the nation.

I have always been a "workaholic" in the sense that I push to always go above and beyond. As Jim Rohn states, "Always do more than what you get paid for. It makes you a valuable person." I volunteered to work every Saturday (meanwhile, others often complained if they had to work two in a row) for months at a time. I never complained* and did any assignment given to me.

While I was a driver, I was still attending school full-time. I pushed on to attend school as a full-time student during my entire five years with A.D.M. As a driver, I would study and do assignments while waiting to load or while unloading. Pulling out my textbook, I would lay it and my notebook across the fender of the trailer while unloading the product. Luckily, the unloading process was passive – hook up a hose, open a valve, turn on the pump, and let the good times roll.

I picked up a habit called no extra time (N.E.T.) from Tony Robbins during this time. No extra time* is the idea of working extra things into the time you already have committed elsewhere. While driving, I would dedicate this time to learning through audio courses and lectures. While unloading, I would study or complete textbook assignments. While working at A.D.M. (driving), I listened to hundreds of hours of self-improvement and self-development audio lessons. It was my "university on wheels," as so many high performers refer to it.

If I was in line somewhere – I had a book in my hand. Especially so when donating plasma. For years I donated plasma twice a week at a local plasma collection bank. Over my donating life, I have given plasma more than 350 times. The process typically took a couple of hours, and I benefited immensely from the time. I read numerous books and studied several school text chapters while donating plasma. It was a N.E.T. win but also a personal win – helping others while improving myself.

I loved driving, but deep down, I desired more. I wanted to grow – after about nine months of driving full-time – an office position opened in the trucking terminal for a night dispatcher. The position posting stated a bachelors was required, and I was still wrapping up an associate, but applied nonetheless. *

SILVER LININGS

• • •

- We must always bet on ourselves. Despite not having a college degree – I still had the confidence and belief that I could not only perform that role well – but that I would get offered the role with enough preparation.
- "No extra time" has been a critical learning element throughout the last decade of my life. If I am commuting anywhere – I have an audiobook or audio lesson on. From languages to leadership, it is all available in an audio format; benefit from it! When you pull into work and hear your colleague's music on blast – smile knowing that promotion will be yours.

Career Growth

was called in for an interview. I take my career very seriously, and even though this was an entry-level position, I arrived wearing nice dress clothes fitted with a tie. I walked into the waiting room and sat down with others also interviewing for the role. I scanned the room, gauging the competition. Simply based on physical presentation alone, I was confident I had the job secured. Others were in jeans, polos, and unshaven.

I had prepared and strongly desired this role. I was called in for the interview and sat down with the hiring manager and the human resources manager. Spending the previous week researching the role and preparing for role-specific interview questions – I crushed the interview. I was unstoppable; at the end of the interview, as I was walking out of the room, the hiring manager told me to stop. He had just now reviewed my resume. "You drive for us"? he asked. Responding affirmatively, he claimed, "I have never met a driver like you."

I knew at that Moment that despite having my CDL, I wasn't a driver. Despite wanting to be a mechanic, I wasn't a mechanic. I was simply on an adventure-seeking growth and experience – the next week, I was invited on my next adventure as a dispatcher. *

SILVER LININGS

• • •

- Preparation for and working towards what is consciously desired in life often leads to manifesting that desire more than those we do not prepare for.

Hard Work and Self Growth

The night dispatcher role was very much "sink or swim." There was no onboarding or training. There was no manual or process for learning the role. I was to shadow another colleague for a few days and then be thrown right into the hot seat. Night dispatch directed all terminals and many national operations throughout after hours. Creating bills of lading, tracking equipment, assigning equipment, monitoring loading, deliveries, handling customer calls, and extinguishing logistical fires were all job duties.

It was fast-paced, and the role operated 24/7/365 without skipping a beat. There were commonly 2-3 calls on hold, with another call in and a few drivers waiting in front of the desk. This role truly turned me into a multitasking master. Despite the tasking job, I still worked to grow, improve, and learn something new each day. I volunteered to cover holiday shifts. At one point during my nightshift journey, I worked 27 days without a day off in conjunction with 90+ hour work weeks.

Nonetheless, I still conquered four courses a semester

and graduated with a 4.0 on my associate's degree. I was hungry and excited for all of the progress and potential in my life. In reality, I was a single father, working nightshift and attending community college. In my mind, I was a superhero with the most important job in the world (I may have been borderline delusional, but that delusion pushed me to conquer all obstacles).

Within six months, I had developed a training manual for the role. * I was promoted to transportation dispatcher and moved to the day shift. I was given my own desk and my own terminal of drivers to dispatch all over the nation. It was much more of the same introduction – trial by fire after shadowing another colleague in the role. The zest and sense of adventure I brought to the new role never ceased. I learned as much as I could and always tried to improve my ability. I worked to help others to the best of my capability – always volunteering to take extra responsibility. I continued working the night desk as well when they were shorthanded. Never* turning down the opportunity to go above the normal call of duty.

During this time, I missed the allure of the open road and an audiobook. I took up a part-time role driving a truck on Saturdays over the road. I would leave Saturday and spend the night in Indiana after delivering to a warehouse. My daughter also tagged along on several of these journeys – there isn't much that compares to family bonding on the road.

My daughter and I at a truck stop

SILVER LININGS

• • •

- I have found that consistently going above and beyond develops a reputation as a go-to among colleagues. This reputation is very valuable in an organization and opens doors that might otherwise have been closed. Trust that those at the top of their class (or office) are getting attention (seen or unseen) from others. Go the extra mile

Rental Property

While living at the trailer and focusing on self-improvement – I became focused on building financial stability. I had always feared not being able to feed or support my daughter and dreaded the thought of living payday to payday. Several books I read had shared avenues to develop a financial foundation, and I was determined to put them to use. My cost of living at the time was minimal. We had struggled enough to adapt to living well below our means. On a 40K salary, I was able to max out my 401k ($18K) and still save some each month.

I tried to build wealth wherever I was able. Donating plasma brought in additional income, all of which I invested into the stock market. I had always wanted to get into real estate and began a rigorous study of that industry. I learned several important skills, such as negotiating a purchase and navigating commercial loans. Somewhere along the journey, I built confidence to purchase, renovate, and rent out a residential home. I had a budget in mind of $40,000 – which is not much at all for purchasing a home and remodeling it.

I searched for a couple of months, reviewing different properties. I finally found one in Warrensburg, IL. It was about a block from the town school and was in an ideal area for raising a growing family. The house was falling apart, but it had strong bones. I negotiated the price from 45K to 20K. In hindsight, I am sure I lucked out in this transaction. The seller needed cash quickly.

I financed the purchase with a commercial loan and added an additional $15,000 for renovation supplies and tools.

I researched tenant laws, rental property requirements, and other applicable regulations and laws. I did a complete walkthrough of the property and made a list of what legally needed renovating and what cosmetically needed enhancement. With the help of my brother and father to assist with the heavy lifting, the entire home was a do-it-yourself project. *

I learned how to mix and apply mortar to resurface the basement. Ripping out the new carpet, I found the entire house had sturdy hardwood floors. I got a book from the library on refinishing hardwood and watched several training videos on the subject. Renting several sanders and purchasing piles of sandpaper, I refinished every floor in the house. Installed new ceiling tiles, new vinyl flooring, new windows, stairs, and wall paneling. I did outsource some plumbing and the siding job to a reliable contractor. Yet, I still stuck around and learned how to do those jobs while they were working.

It was a hefty project, but we succeeded and did it within budget. The neighbors were so happy that the neighborhood "eyesore" had been spruced up. They came over while I was doing an open house and offered potential new residents snacks. Within two weeks of listing the house, I had secured a 3-year lease at $1,100 month. The ROI on my first property project has paid for itself in full while bringing strong cash flow through the years. * This win pushed me to continue making intentional financial decisions that have led me to a debt-free and financially stress-free life.

SILVER LININGS

• • •

- When we apply ourselves to something wholeheartedly – we often find it to be much easier than anticipated. When you are all in on a project, you tend to find resourcefulness that helps you push through.
- There are points in our lives where we must take the leap and take a risk on ourselves. Diving into something outside of the comfort zone may lead to a return on capital and new skills.

Dad helping tear down the ceiling, work in progress

Seeking Opportunity

volunteered to be the chairman of the location's safety board. I eventually won the seat and began leading meetings. I gained valuable public speaking skills and project management experience. At the same time, I was still keeping my nose to the grindstone, attending college full-time, now working on my bachelor's.

About two years into my role as a transportation dispatcher – I felt I was ready for the next step. I had recently been passed up for internal promotion – informed that it was because I did not have the college requirements. I knew that wasn't the true verdict but accepted it as it was given. *

I put myself through rigorous self-improvement regimens. College, gym fitness, reading a book every two weeks, taking extra skill-specific courses, and more. I had self-taught myself enough excel know-how to pass a Microsoft certification test. I knew I was ready for more responsibility in my career. As Les Brown says, "I WAS HUNGRY"!

I felt I had hit a glass ceiling within the dispatch team and set my sights elsewhere. I applied internally for several roles and started growing my network. ADM is a gigantic corporation with several business units and more than

30,000 employees – the company was seething with opportunity. Still, on a never-ending self-improvement kick, I had heard from several high-performing professionals that a mentor was vital to success. Not willing to settle for just any mentor – I traveled to the top of our business unit. * A dispatcher was fairly low on the internal totem pole. It was outside of my comfort zone to approach anyone and ask to be mentored. Pushing through fear, I asked the vice president of the business unit to mentor me. He didn't hesitate to accept the request.

SILVER LININGS

• • •

- Continue to grow and learn to venture regularly outside of the comfort zone. If you shoot for the sun and miss – you will still land among the stars.

Mentorship

Over the course of a few months, I met with the company leader for mentorship meetings. We both shared our backgrounds and professional goals for the future. He had a very inspiring career story. Beginning as a shop employee in a relatively small terminal – he worked his way up the corporate ladder rung by rung. Accepting more responsibility and chasing growth opportunities – he found his way to the vice president title with old fashioned work ethic and a desire for self-growth.

He expressed that he was in the phase of his career in which passing on knowledge (mentorship) was a value he could bring to others. * I learned several valuable lessons during our time together. I learned the importance that soft skills play in leadership roles. That emotional intelligence is more important for a leader than technical know-how. I learned that the foundation for career growth within a large organization is relationships. He shared the importance of fostering relationships and never burning bridges if at all possible. Reverting to his story of growing from a shop employee to the Vice President, you never know who may be wherein a decade or two. Another valuable learning was the importance of picking up the phone. In an area in which everyone sends e-mails, a phone call is a rare and critical tool.

SILVER LININGS

• • •

- When you focus on bringing value to others, you will inevitably find value within yourself and for yourself.

Opportunity Seeks the Prepared

W hen you focus on self-growth, opportunity has a strange way of finding you. Not much longer after I began mentoring with the company leader, an exciting opportunity fell into my lap. The company had won a bid on new business in New York. They needed a dispatcher onsite temporarily to learn the route and driver capabilities. I was presently managing northeast drivers and was given the first option to fly to New York for a few weeks to develop a dispatch structure.

Naturally, I jumped at the opportunity and found myself at the airport a week later. I had tied up all of my loose ends and ensured my daughter was taken care of while I was away. I was out of my mind excited (this is a trend when you make the decision to live in gratitude) to board the plane. It was my first-ever airplane ride. At age 25, I was acting like a 12-year-old at the airport. I gasped at how big the airport was itself – my first flight ever was out of Chicago O'Hare. If you were there, I was the guy who took ages in the security check because he wasn't prepared to take off his boots.

Boarding the plane, I had to have been the happiest passenger in coach. * It was just like the movies – the flight attendant gave us the spiel – keep your seat belts on and how to use an oxygen mask. Shortly after the plane began its ascent – I was flying! I snapped as many pictures of the take-off as I could and just as many during the night landing. I was in awe.

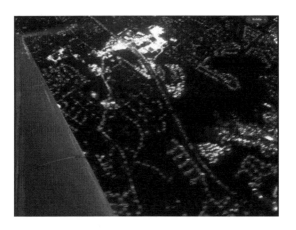

Landing in Albany, NY

SILVER LININGS

● ● ●

- Life has so so many gifts to offer that does not require first class to enjoy.

The Grindstone

F or the next few weeks, I navigated the start-up operations of the transportation terminal. We onboarded a dozen drivers while training them to be safe and efficient. I learned the shipment routes and streamlined location processes. Working with the corporate recruiter who was also at the location short-term during start-up – I caught wind that the location was interviewing for a terminal manager.

I tossed the idea around in my head, considering myself for the role. I considered the personal implications and the professional opportunity. I convinced myself that it was the best move for my family and me. I had no doubt in my mind that this was my time to showcase my skills and prove to company leadership that I was the best fit for the role.

I prepared endlessly for terminal manager responsibilities. * I learned the ins and outs of the local terminal and began creating daily project reports to share with leadership. I reported on the status of the location and areas of the business needing improvement. I learned more about shop management, food-grade wash bays, food-grade shipping, pneumatic operations (the fleet was compiled of pneumatic trailers), driver management, and much more. I was a learning machine while onsite, and I did not hesitate to demonstrate it.

A pneumatic trailer pulled by a day cab tractor.

With the daily project reports, I developed project plans and compiled data analysis of valuable location level metrics. I built rapport with the local team in all areas of the business while moving myself into the good graces of higher-level leaders. A few weeks turned into a few more weeks. I heard through the "grapevine" that many thought I would be a good fit for a location manager. When the interview rounds began, I was offered the chance to throw my hat in the ring. I completed my application and polished a cover letter and resume.

The interview included some of the most difficult interview questions of my life. It was behavioral based with questions aimed at revealing the true level of knowledge regarding the role responsibilities. Questions such as "How would you manage a driver's portfolio in regard to compliance" or "From most important to least, tell us ten items critical to developing a transportation terminal" – leave little room to fake your way through the interview. I walked in with extreme confidence, having studied, researched, and prepared for the interview. This correlated to walking out feeling that I had given the best interview I was capable of.

For the next week, all signs pointed to me being

offered the role if I truly wanted it. My hometown company mentor called the next week. He wanted to have a serious discussion regarding the role in New York. His intentions were to ensure that I considered the potential life-changing pivot from all angles. He informed me that the company would be bringing me back home to have time to think it over. *

SILVER LININGS

• • •

- Touching on preparation again. Preparation for the known events in life is critical to success. Few people give a world-class speech without first considering their words. I am not aware of any actors or actresses that can perform in a blockbuster without first rehearsing. I have always considered the "4 P's" throughout my career. Preparation. Prevents. Poor. Performance.

- At the time, I felt I was ready to dive headfirst into the new role. Down the road, I can appreciate the wisdom the company leader had in ensuring I was fully prepared and committed.

Family Discussions

When one has a family to care for, one cannot simply make life-changing decisions without including them. I knew what I desired – I wanted to get away from what we had known and reset in a new area. The potential for self-improvement seemed unlimited in New York. The only two opinions that truly would have an impact on me were my brother and daughter.

My first and favored plan was to convince them both to relocate to NY with me. Unfortunately, that idea was quickly and repetitively shot down. My brother did not want to leave his comfort zone, and my daughter couldn't bear the thought of being without other family members and friends. I let the dilemma stew for a while before considering alternate realities. I knew I could override her wishes and pull the father's trump card. But I also knew that she would never forgive me and likely suffer while in NY.

My daughter was ten at the time. I recalled what my life had been like around that age. I remembered the emotions I struggled with, along with what I felt like not having a family to lean on. As I combatted this – the universe worked to support my growth and ensure everyone remained happy. * My daughters' Grandparents offered to take temporary guardianship of her while I was working. This would enable me to travel and allow my daughter to remain with family and friends. I would keep full custody while having the ability to visit and reach her anytime. I would give my brother the title to the trailer we lived in as well as give him an avenue to support himself.

SILVER LININGS

• • •

- It is interesting the way the universe creates a path for us when the desire is strong enough.

Brotherly Support and Deep Ditches

I paid for my brother to go through the same CDL course I had. He enjoyed it, and after earning his CDL, he was offered his first role as an over-the-road trucker. He would spend a few weeks at a time in the truck and return home for a few days. He drove contently for a few months – then winter arrived.

My brother had never driven, nor had he been trained to drive in extreme weather conditions. That winter, Michigan had a brutal blizzard that led to white-out conditions. My brother found himself traversing the roads in an old beat-up Freightliner (semi-truck) pulling a 53-foot trailer during those conditions. He was looking for a place to safely stop, but before he found it, he lost control of the tractor and jackknifed through a guard rail into a ditch.

75,000 lbs. of semi-truck barreled downhill onto a small side road. As he came to, he was suspended by the seatbelt and unable to free himself. The truck cab had come separated from the frame – and on its side, he was unable to reach his phone or unlatch his seatbelt. The engine stalled, and he had no heat in the cab. Laying there for nearly twelve hours – no one found him until the next morning due to the blizzard.

He survived the incident wearing a neck brace and covered in bruised for the next month or so. Following the incident, he has had trouble with feeling safe while driving. He refuses to drive a semi-truck to this day and dropped his CDL. * When traveling together, he has difficultly allowing others to drive on the interstate. Thankfully, he had saved up enough while driving during that sprint to support himself in the low-maintenance trailer for quite some time. *

SILVER LININGS

• • •

- Trauma in our lives has a way of preventing us from not only moving forward – but of limiting our potential. It took several years for my brother to get comfortable driving again. During that time, who knows what he may have missed due to the fear of driving.

- Living below one's means is a surefire way to live financially comfortably. The stress of financial burden in our nation is devastating – it can greatly be reduced by eliminating the feeling of needing more and by finding happiness and gratitude for the abundance present now.

A post-incident photo

Servant Leadership

With everything in place, I accepted the job offer and set sails for New York. The company relocated me – helping with relocation costs (a new level of "fancy" for a kid from the city slums). I found a small but quaint cottage for rent about fifteen minutes from the office. The daily 30-minute commute was solid enough to get some motivational audio into me each day.

I doubled down on my growth efforts while in New York. I applied myself vigorously to the manager role. During my time at the terminal, we grew from zero revenue to seven figures. Our employee retention remained at 100% for well over a year (a unicorn in the trucking industry), and our force continued grow. Our growth and retention rates didn't stem from luck – I treated the team like humans. I approached every interaction and each day from a servitude approach. I sincerely believe that the servant leadership style is unequal when it is genuine. I would include all levels of colleagues in our decision-making as much as possible. I would ask drivers and terminal operations colleagues for advice on all things big and small. I hand-wrote personalized letters to colleagues for holidays – all thirty of them. I could be found at the terminal 2-3-4 AM many days, helping others get a head start on their responsibilities. I always aimed to set an example and never complained.

When in the presence of colleagues, I was always smiling unless the situation required otherwise. I concretely feel that the leaders' emotions impact everyone on the team – positive breeds positive just as much as negative breeds negative. I slept on a small camping cot in the office a handful of nights to conquer my self-set goal deadlines. I invited colleagues to attend the gym with me and always supported their self-improvement while trying to set an example myself.

My approach may have been unorthodox, but having read numerous leadership books (Simon Sinek to John Maxwell), I knew that as a 25-year-old managing a team averaging twice my age, I had to be extraordinary to be taken seriously. * Early into the adventure, we had several team meetings in which I told the team I was there for them. That my job was to improve their lives and make their working experience better – that I was available for them 24/7/365. I had zero management experience, but I knew what I had always desired from a leader and tried to offer the team exactly that. *

I wasn't chasing money or prestige – I was seeking experience, self-growth, and a platform to grow upon – I found it in New York. Over the couple of years I spent with the terminal, we grew exponentially. We also navigated several highs and lows together. I led the team through a terrible plant fatality that shook our terminal. I led the team through the entire pandemic as a group of "essential" workers. I didn't portray myself as a "boss" but as a "leader." I had my CDL and would drive with colleagues to deliver to customers. I equipped the same uniforms and same gear the team was required to wear daily – I was the only terminal manager in the company to order himself work uniforms.

Myth busted: *You can be professional and encourage a joyful work environment at the same time.*

I would scrub the wash bay, put air in tires in the shop, help lift, help clean, vacuum, take out the trash – all in the service of the team. This servant-leader approach was, in my opinion, hands down the largest variable in creating and maintaining a highly effective and strongly knit team. * Our first full year operating together as a unit and as being the youngest terminal at the time – our operating margins outpaced all other senior terminals.

SILVER LININGS

• • •

- Early on, while transitioning into the management position, there was some pushback from older colleagues. This can be found in all industries and all roles, even within the military. I recall a story from my father about an inexperienced "college kid" stepping into leading a unit. The stigma will always be there, and the only way around it is to prove your mettle. Contribute to the front line and perform the duties considered grunt work. This inevitably earns respect with time.

- During my time as an employee at different locations, I had experienced leaders that had a deficit in leadership knowledge. From my Walmart manager laughing at me, my Sears manager laying off an entire team with no emotion, and my Mack manager being indifferent to the hostile work environment – I knew who I wouldn't be and decided in advance who I would be.

- Servant leadership is putting your team before you in all things. Words will not earn respect – actions will.

Extreme Personal Growth

W hile working full-time as the terminal manager – I was also continuing my education as a full-time student. I tried to live by Jim Rohn's quote, "work harder on yourself than you do your job."* This one was a struggle because I worked extremely hard on my job. Yet, I pushed myself to improve in all areas I was able to. This began with streamlining my day today.

I purchased a "sonic-boom" alarm clock and set it up at the other end of the cottage. Each night I would turn on the alarm set for 4:30 AM. I would prepare for the next day by laying out clothes and preparing meals. Each morning I had a morning ritual* – splashing cold water onto my face. I grabbed my gym bag, lunch bag, and work portfolio. I would exercise from 5-7, doing an hour of cardio, 45 minutes of anaerobic focus, and 15 minutes doing a guided meditation.

I read a book while performing the cardio (remember Tony Robbins NET?). While on the stair master, elliptical, or stationary bike, I would read through numerous technical and non-fiction books. Turning on classical music in my headphones – I would zone out and dial into the book. The lineup included books such as professional certification study guides and all books under the umbrella of self-improvement. Time management, goal setting, communication, body language, public speaking, personal finance, business finance, spirituality, and so much more. I was pushing through a serious amount of literature in that NY gym. It equated to about two books a month.

I recorded several "personalized" guided meditations that helped me visualize a future I designed. I included my ideal financial situation, education, dream career, and more. The power of meditation and visualization is hard to explain to the unindoctrinated* – all I can say is if you haven't, you owe it to yourself to try it.

After my work shift (which never really ended as I received calls every hour), I did schoolwork. I eventually earned my bachelor's degree and began working on my next goal, an MBA degree. (When looking back – I still can hardly believe I made it from school drop out to earning a bachelor's). I earned several professional certifications as the desire for learning and applying that learning became internalized (Google helps with acronyms – I use it regularly). I earned the APICS CSCP, PMP, CTP, and others that required extensive study. I joined groups of professionals and loved the journey of learning. I even signed up for courses at a local community college to gain other skills such as photoshopping and website creation. My desire to grow and learn was endless.

SILVER LININGS

• • •

- Working harder on yourself than you do your job is a simple concept – the more you improve yourself as an individual, the more opportunity that will open up to you. Maintaining the status quo and not learning new skills would have likely led to me still living in a trailer to this day.

- A morning ritual is one of my personal favorite self-discipline actions. Starting the morning with a ritual that primes you for the coming day is very powerful.

- My first introduction to meditation was at an alternative school. I was extremely skeptical when we began. A year later, meditation had become a staple in my life and improved, among other things – my stability and self-awareness.

Destiny Strikes Again

J anuary 1st, 2021, I was taking a week off from work to drive home to see family. I was excited to see my daughter, brother, and others. Needless to say – it is a haul from New York to Illinois! I began the trek on New Year's Day, leaving my cottage in the morning. Making my way through Pennsylvania, a snowstorm began. I didn't see the black ice that had formed on the road.

I lost control of the truck, and the vehicle did a 360 while barreling 60 MPH into the ditch. The truck rolled as I clenched and repeated "no, no, no" in fear. I found my-self lying on the driver's side door, the driver's side of the vehicle embedded in the earth. I loosened my seat belt and stood up. The entire I was regaining my awareness, I was shouting at myself, "I'm alive." I could hardly believe it, but I was nearly completely unscathed. I tried to lift open the passenger side door and climb out. The door was too heavy to lift at the awkward angle I found myself in.

Finding my cell phone, I called 911 – following the panic call, I saw some smoke coming through the dash. Extreme adrenaline mode kicked at the sight of the smoke. At the same time, a passerby pulled over and ran over the truck that lay sideways in the ditch. He saw me struggling and helped me get out of the truck. With the door held open, I stood on the steering wheel, climbed out of the top of the truck, and jumped off into the snow. The gentleman was in a sweatshirt and jeans, looking me over and asking if I was alright.

I was, I checked all over for any sign of injury and found nothing apparent aside from minor impact soreness. The man waited with me for the first responders. I was grateful he had stopped – a dozen others had driven past with little consideration. * He offered to let me sit in his car, but I rejected politely. He had already helped enough. He handed me the beanie from his head as a first responder pulled up to the scene. The gentleman wished me luck and told me to stay warm. He was walking away and driving off before I even had the chance to get his name.

I was so hyped up on adrenaline that I hadn't even realized I was in a t-shirt in a winter storm. Refusing medical attention, the tow truck arrived and gave me a lift to a nearby truck stop in Snowshoe, PA. They had some decent chicken and cool trinkets for sale. As I sat in the back of the truck stop, eating coleslaw – I dwelled in my thoughts for hours. I was sure as I slid down the interstate that I was going to die. It reminded me, in a very potent form, how frail life can be. *

Thankfully, I did not pass that day and was gifted another opportunity to continue this journey. I recalled all the people that had driven by and among them the one man who had stopped and given me the beanie from his head. I felt a deep need to do more with my life. As I sat there, I meditated on my day and the life choices that had brought me to that truck stop.

I decided then and there that I wouldn't waste another day. * I would work on myself, not for only myself, but to help others. I would give back to those who had helped me and sought to help others. I would share my story and work to shine a light on a path that others may not know exists.

Just as when we are children – we are unable to see more than others allow us to; when we are adults, we often do not see more than what our lives have limited us to. Often the only thing that is wrong with our lives is the way we think about it – change the way we think, and we can change our lives.

Flipped my truck on New Years

SILVER LININGS

• • •

It is common to be a bystander. To allow events to occur or to dismiss others and their needs. Our world needs more of the uncommon. We need those who are willing to truly act selflessly and aid others in need.

- I have noticed a pattern in our society in which the mortality characteristic of life is overlooked until the final Moments of life. I sincerely believe that those who accept that our life as we know it is not eternal – will find themselves living each day at a higher and more fulfilled level than those who do not.
- Facing the prospect of not being offered another day creates an urgency to explore, adventure, live happily, and add to others. Decide today to live every remaining day with zest and a mission.

New Adventures

I n July of 2021, I made the decision to shake things up. I was at a point in my corporate career in which I was unfulfilled and unchallenged. I had hit the proverbial glass ceiling in our business unit, at least until the director was promoted or retired. I put a hard stop on myself when I found myself chasing a raise rather than self-expansion. Knowledge and new experience had become my preferred form of compensation, especially so after my car accident.

I began looking for an opportunity in areas where winter was obsolete (Design your best life!). I personally experience a huge sink in motivation and energy when the winter season arrives. The brutally cold temperature often reduces my ability to jog outdoors and the sun disappearing sooner is never fun. Luckily, I stumbled across Arizona!

The average temperature in the winter months doesn't get below sixty degrees. The clock stays the same through all seasons, and the new adventures are abundant. I had never been further west than Missouri and knew the change would be awesome. The universe sharing its support again – helped me land the perfect opportunity to help support the life change.

Leaving a Fortune 100 company that would have

provided a stable, secure paycheck for life – I found an exciting growth opportunity with a logistics start-up and took a leap of faith. * The company, Fresh Freight LLC, is family-owned and operated – they started fleet operations in late 2019 and brought me on to help develop the fleet.

Helping develop a fleet program from the bottom-up is extremely exciting. I am still navigating the MBA full-time and wrapping up this small project you are reading in conjunction with trying to level up some each day.

I hope to get the opportunity to continue being a student of life and to try new growth and improvement practices to share with others in the future. For now, I am starting to share some of these experiences through my newly formed company.

SILVER LININGS

• • •

- Taking a leap of faith has been a requirement to experience exponential improvements in life. Do not ever hesitate to bet on yourself – you do not want to be the individual the looks back thinking "what-if".

Evolve and Elevate LLC

Returning from my week off and the universe slapping me in the face with a sign to pivot my life – the time to level up and help others came. I incorporated my own company, Evolved and Elevated LLC that I decided would be used as an umbrella for my mission to improve myself and others. I began a podcast and blog, which are in their infancy at evolvedandelevated.com. My pledge is to do a podcast season each year that shares self-development information I have found impactful. To write a book on a topic around self-development or skill improvement every handful of years. And to simply commit to better myself so I can better help others.

As such, a majority percentage of revenue generated from this book and future books will be shared with the numerous entities that helped me through life when I was struggling. Among those, a very special thanks to the salvation army, food pantries, and Northeast community fund. As well as to our country's leadership for developing programs to help citizens who need assistance. For helping a struggling father feed his daughter and assisting an ambitious young adult in pursuing college. I will gladly pay taxes for my remaining years, knowing it is going to support others out there that need a leg up so they may also thrive and run with the rest of the pack.

At the end of this book, you will find a "World changer declaration of growth." It is a pledge I hope you will seriously consider no matter your background, age, or past. Our ability to change the world begins with the decision to change ourselves. Before you sign (or do not) remember that this life is finite and the time to grow, change, help, build, and improve is not unlimited. I hope that no one will ever find themselves barreling at 60 MPH into a ditch wishing they had done more with their life – it is not a good feeling.

Following the pledge, in the remainder of the book, you will find numerous tips, lists, and avenues for success that I have found valuable, such as self-development books, personal finance, career tips, personal fitness, goal setting, time management, visualization, and meditations, among others.

But remember, be a student, not a follower. Don't pick up everything you see lying around because it worked for someone else. Navigate it, decipher it, research it, and make up your own mind about it.

<u>You are The Hero of Your Own Story</u>

World Changer Declaration of Action

I pledge to take individual action and personal ownership to improve the world.

I pledge to seek self-improvement and lift myself into a higher level of performance. I will devote my time and energy to improving my life in all areas.

I pledge not to blame others. I will take full responsibility for all of my actions and all of my life results.

I pledge not to complain. I will solve my problems and improve my situation as I move forward.

I pledge to always love myself and to appreciate who I have become. I will have gratitude for the lessons learned in my past.

I swear to apply my mind and body to improve the world.

I swear to respect others and to have compassion for others in all walks of life. I will hold no grudges against anyone.

I swear that I will find and pursue my personal mission. I will live my life to the fullest each day.

I swear that I will help lift up another whenever I am able.

I, _____, DECLARE MYSELF A WORLD CHANGER.

Resources for Self-Improvement

This section is a small compilation of information I have found useful in my personal journey. I hope you will find some of the content useful as you work to develop your own lists and tips. As you continue your journey towards self-growth and helping improve our world – I hope you will consider sharing your growth journey story with me at jakefry@evolvedandelevated.com.

I will continue to share with you any new lessons I learn through my blog and podcast at evolvedandelevated.com.

I wish you all the best and strong winds!

DISCLAIMER: Nothing within this book is physical nor financial advice. I am not a healthcare professional nor a finance professional. Please do your personal due diligence and consult a professional for guidance as needed.

My Personal Top 20 Book List

1. *As a Man Thinketh* by James Allen
2. *Becoming Supernatural: How Common People Are Doing the Uncommon* by Dr. Joe Dispenza
3. *Winning: The Unforgiving Race to Greatness* by Tim S. Grover
4. *12 Rules for Life: An Antidote to Chaos* by Jordan B. Peterson
5. *Extreme Ownership: How US Navy Seals Lead and Win* by Jocko Willink and Leif Babin
6. *The Richest Man in Babylon* by George S. Clason
7. *The 7 Habits of Highly Effective People* by Stephen R. Covey
8. *The Power of Positive Thinking* by Norman Vincent Peale
9. *The Bible* – The Bible includes numerous strategies for success for both the religious as well as the non-religious.
10. *Deep Work* by Cal Newport
11. *Tools of Titans: The Tactics, Routines, and Habits of Billionaires* by Tim Ferris

12. *Money Master the Game:* **7 *Simples Steps to Financial Freedom*** by Tony Robbins
13. *Mastery* by Robert Greene
14. *ALIEN Thinking: The Unconventional Path to Breakthrough Ideas* by Cyril Bouquet, Jean-Louis Barsoux, Michael Wade
15. *Automatic Millionaire* by David Bach
16. *Million Dollar Habits* by Brian Tracy
17. *Can't Hurt Me: Master Your Mind and Defy the Odds* by David Goggins
18. *The Compound Effect* by Darren Hardy
19. *Wishes Fulfilled* by Dr. Wayne W. Dyer
20. *Atomic Habits: An Easy & Proven Way to Build Good Habits & Break Bad Ones* by James Clear

Personal Finance

92' Mazda: $2900 including registration

Financial security is a stressor that is at the forefront of most individuals list of hardships. For myself, being raised in poverty has given me a head start in regard to developing the one skill I had found foundational to creating financial independence. Frugality and living below one's means are those foundational skills. You may be thinking "frugality" is not a skill. However, in a nation that is up to its gills in debt; I would argue otherwise.

Frugality is simply a fiscally conscious form of

resourcefulness. It is hands down the most significant variable in my personal financial life. Below are examples of frugality in my life followed by more financial tips I have had success with.

Frugality in My Life

"There is no dignity quite so impressive, and no independence quite so important, as living within your means."

- Calvin Coolidge

- 99% of my personal wardrobe is from thrift stores.
- I lived in a trailer for years even while owning residential rental properties.
- Until I had reached a level of financial comfort, I drove vehicles that cost less than $3k. Often vehicles older than I am!
- I graduated with a 4-year degree debt free due to working full time while attending school and paying for each course as I progressed.
- I have always tried to live by a "no-nonsense" debt philosophy. If I go into debt, it must be for personal growth or researched investments (such as rental property).

Finances

"The rich invest their money and spent what is left;
the poor spend their money and invest what is left"

– Jim Rohn

- **Invest in yourself!** I have found my ability to earn to correlate to the time and funds I invest in myself. For example, formal education and CDL training.
- **Automate your savings.** I never would have been able to keep my savings and investing consistency without automating the process. By automating the process, in the early years, $18,000 out of a $40,000 salary was sent to my 401k only because I did not see that money first. It was automated to be withdrawn straight from my paycheck – what you do not see, you will not miss.
- **Earn hard, Save hard**, **Invest hard**. *We simply cannot save money without earning money. We cannot invest money without saving money*. Work on yourself to increase your value to the marketplace to earn hard. Automate your savings and save hard. Invest your savings intelligently.

- **Invest with intention.** I began managing my personal portfolio only after doing significant research and focused learning. If there is not time in your day to do the learning – considering hiring a professional to guide your investments. No matter what path you take, be intentional in your investing.
- **Passive income**. In the long game towards financial freedom passive income is a necessity. I personally have had success with real estate and dividend stocks – research and find investment channels that will bring you passive income.
- **Beware of vices**. Vices can lead to a huge money pit and time syphon. In my life, I have tackled a couple – most recently was a bout with gambling. During my time as a dispatcher, the company had a Christmas party at a local bowling alley. The bowling alley had video gambling slots. (They are literally everywhere in Decatur, IL.) I had never played nor had the desire to play – until a colleague asked me to join him. I slid in twenty dollars and won several hundred. This led to a nasty gambling addiction over the next year. I found myself with these machines and their flashing lights with exciting sound effects far too often. The only way I was able to conquer the vice was to eliminate all possibility of it occurring. I left my money cards at home except when needed. I never carried cash and would intentionally steer clear of locations that contained

video slots. While I understand that some vices are not as easily "eliminated" – it is vital to recognize that no matter the vice (drugs, alcohol, gambling) will undoubtedly take away from our potential best self. Do your best to avoid developing it in the first place – if you do struggle with a vice, know there is help available.

Careers

"Nothing will work unless you do."

- Maya Angelou

Almost looks legit!

We spend a significant amount of our life within the workplace. Our time dedicated to our careers must be intentional and growth focused. I began working fulltime at sixteen after dropping out of high school and have not stopped running since. The early years were messy and not focused – the following are some insights I have found valuable from my experiences to date.

Do not ever underestimate the value of paying dues. Each step in our career paths has something to offer in regard to personal growth, skills, or relationships. Here is an overview of my personal career trajectory with financial insights and lessons learned. It is definitely not a straight line!

TITLE | AGE | WAGE | LESSONS LEARNED

Construction work | 16 | $10/HR | Work Ethic
D.S.P. | 18 | $8/HR | Gratitude for life's basic gifts
Walmart Technician | 19 | $9/HR | Shop skills, humility
Sears Technician | 20 | $10/HR | Shop skills, emotional intelligence
Mack Technician | 21 | $12/HR | Advance shop skills, blind optimism
Truck Driver | 23 | $21/HR | Patience, respect for highway heroes
Night Dispatch | 24 | $18/HR | Multitasking, performing under pressure
Dispatcher | 24 | $21/HR | Strategy, project management, data analytics
Terminal Manager | 25 | $42/HR | Leadership skills, high-level industry skills
Fleet Manager | 28 | $39/HR | TBD

The decreases in wages throughout the journey were

balanced by other benefits. Benefits such as more time with family, growth opportunity, and personal happiness. In moving from truck driver to night dispatcher I took a loss in wages. However, I took a win in home-time. In the move from terminal manager to fleet manager I took a loss in wages. However, I took a win in personal happiness and growth potential. The moral of the story? If we search, we will find valuable lessons in all roles within our careers. If we are unable to find these lessons – we must consider seeking them elsewhere.

Career Tips

"Choose a job you love, and you will never have to work a day in your life."

—Confucius

- **Always maintain professionalism.** Our careers are serious and must be taken seriously. There is a time in place for silly in the workplace – be sure you know when that time is rather than assuming.
- **Do not gossip.** Never say anything about a colleague that you would not say directly to them. In the workplace, gossip is one thing that will never remain a secret. It will also garner you a rather poor reputation.
- **Do not burn bridges.** You never truly know when you may need the help of another. Keep your network and relationships strong.
- **Do more than you are paid for.** Always seek the next opportunity. Ask to help others when able. Leadership is always seeking go-getters and those that bring relentlessness to the workplace.

- **Have grit, be disciplined.** If one wishes to rise to the heights of the marketplace – one must be prepared to hunker down and work. Be prepared for the grind at different career stages.
- **Mentorship, mentorship, mentorship.** Having someone to help us grow towards our desired future role is priceless. Seek a mentor in different stages of the career. When you have garnered the experience to mentor, pay it forward.
- **Always have compassion.** It is critical to remember that we are all human. Bring compassion to the workplace when it is needed. However, keep in mind that there is a difference between having compassion and being manipulated.

Time Management & Goals

"Lack of direction, not lack of time, is the problem. We all have twenty-four hour days."

- Zig Ziglar

Time is a precious resource – what is expended may never be recouped. The careful planning and use of our available time are a critical component to success. Keep in mind that success is within the eye of the beholder; it is not universal to all individuals. Be sure that time is applied to your personal happiness and success – not another's idea of it.

An important piece to ensure strong use of time is to have a path paved (goals) for future travel. In order to have a successful year it is helpful to plan the year before we live it. Goals are the north star of our ideal future. By designing our ideal future, we can develop goals around the variables we want in our life. Such as a degree, a dream home, or a happy family.

Time Management & Goals Tips

"People are not lazy. They simply have impotent goals—that is, goals that do not inspire them."
— Tony Robbins

- **Develop goals around your desired future.** Goals should represent a surefire path to the life we desire. For example, my personal desire is to earn an PhD in the future. My present goals include earning an MBA and reading literature around my ideal major.
- **Create and track a task list.** Organizing items that must be completed is a serious boon for time management. Very few people have the ability to keep all items in their life managed within the mind. Put it on paper, put it on a calendar, and monitor it regularly.
- **Attack the priority.** Just as our "to-do" list is an important piece of time management; so is focusing on efficient elimination of the to-do items.

Organize and focus on the items that will bring the most value to the mission and goal. Do not push off the harder items for last – attack the priority!

- **Elimination of distraction will improve performance.** We simply cannot think, learn, or produce at a high level while surrounded with distractions. Set aside time to focus with intention. I personally set aside a chunk of time to focus on learning or producing in a closet (weird, I know! But I thrive on weird) with ear plugs in. Also, no phone!

Personal Fitness

"Exercise is king. Nutrition is queen. Put them together, and you've got a kingdom."

– Jack Lalanne

P ersonal fitness is something I personally have struggled with throughout my life. As you know, our society puts significant weight on appearance which often leads to high self-consciousness. The good news is that personal fitness and health is governed by mostly universal rules. Meaning that just about anyone, anywhere, can improve their health.

The two critical items boil down to nutrition (what we eat) and exercise. Changing these two factors in our life, especially from an area of lack, will inevitably begin as a hardship. It begins as a hardship but transforms into a joyful and desired experience. Early on, I found that exercise consistent of rigorous self-torture. I began with trying to run a block and simply doing five push-ups. As time progressed the one block became two, and the five push-ups became ten.

The early battle will be perilous and difficult. It will require perseverance, grit, and blind optimism – the results will take time. But, if you push through, your energy levels, self-confidence, and health benefits will speak for themselves.

Personal Fitness Tips

"Take care of your body. It's the only place you have to live".

– Jim Rohn

- **IMPROVE NUTRITION.** The foods we eat and the beverages we drink are 90% of the battle. I found that improving my personal diet led to significant weight loss and increased health. Remove the known unhealthy items from the diet. By simply removing flour, sugar, and salt we can eliminate most unhealthy items from our diet. I lost well over 100 pounds following the removal of soda, sweets (I loved Reese's), fast food, and baked goods from my diet entirely.

- **Exercise regularly.** Daily if possible. In my personal life I visit the gym 5-7 times per week. I started with humble beginnings several years ago. Remember, it isn't so much knowing where to start, but starting somewhere.

- **Stretch!** Stretching routines are often overlooked. Yet, it is one of the most beneficial practices regarding self-health. Consider a yoga class!

Meditation & Visualization

"Mediation means dissolving the invisible walls that unaware has built"

– Sadhguru

I mentioned that in my personal journey meditation is something that was approached with skepticism. After years of meditating for stress-relief, focus, self-awareness, and future visualization – I now firmly believe it had been a key factor to my self-growth and overall success. I have especially benefited from creating personalized guided meditations that help to visualize my ideal best life.

An indirect impact of meditation has been reducing the control of the ego. It has helped me evolved into an individual that does not live solely for the approval of others. So many live engrossed with what others think of them. They buy a Porsche not for personal fulfillment, but rather for what they believe it will make others think of them. It is critical to live life on our terms in search of our own happiness. Otherwise, we risk leaving this life with no true friends nor ever finding our true self. Advanced meditation has helped me find that true self. I sincerely believe it will do the same for others.

Meditation & Visualization Tips

"You are more productive by doing fifteen minutes of visualization than from sixteen hours of hard labor."

- Abraham Hicks

- **Incorporate meditation.** There are several avenues to try meditation. YouTube has proven to be a reliable and vast collection of valuable information from others across the world. Among that valuable information is guided meditations. Try searching for "beginner meditations".

- **Personalized meditation.** Script, record, and listen to your own designed meditations. Visualize your ideal future a decade from today – perhaps with your successful business or your dream vacation with your family. You will find a sample template at the bottom of my blog at evolvedandelevated.com

- **The mind movie**. I first read about this tool in Dr. Joe Dispenza's book *Becoming Supernatural*. Essentially it is a video of items you wish to manifest in your life. I pieced together one for myself with Microsoft word, images from the internet, and stereo playing a trigger song while a recorded it from my smart phone.

Thank You!

"As we express our gratitude, we must never forget that the highest appreciation is not to utter words, but to live by them."

– John F. Kennedy

I am so very grateful that you have invested precious time to navigate this book. This book has been my first attempt at writing a full-length book. I truly hope that you have found something helpful within the pages. If there was something that resonated (or that could have been better) – please tell me about it! Here are some avenues to share and or connect with me – may all your desires be realized!

Email: jakefry@evolvedandelevated.com
LinkedIn: linkedin.com/in/jakemfry/
Website: evolvedandelevated.com

Made in the USA
Columbia, SC
11 December 2021

50993826R00141